ASSESSING YOUTH WHO HAVE SEXUALLY ABUSED: A PRIMER

DAVID S. PRESCOTT, LICSW

Assessing Youth Who Have Sexually Abused: A Primer

Copyright©2007
David S. Prescott, LICSW

Published by
NEARI Press
70 North Summer Street
Holyoke, MA 01040
413.540.0712

Distributed by
Whitman Distribution
10 Water Street
PO Box 1220
Lebanon, New Hampshire 03766
603.448.0037
800.353.3730

ISBN# 1-929657-27-7

This Primer is dedicated to my family, with thanks for their endless support and encouragement.

I am indebted to David Thornton, Sue Righthand, Robert Prentky, Gail Ryan, Jim Worling, Janis Bremer, Doug Epperson, and all those who are willing to share their work and thoughts with others. I am grateful to Diane Langelier, Rob Longo, and Steve Bengis for their efforts in bringing knowledge and inspiration to others.

ASSESSING YOUTH WHO HAVE SEXUALLY ABUSED: A PRIMER

DAVID S. PRESCOTT, LICSW

Introduction

It is difficult to underestimate the importance of high-quality assessment of youth who have sexually abused. Assessments can guide decisions that affect the development of young people, as well as family growth and community safety. Good assessments can help us to devise treatment strategies and make appropriate placement decisions. However, there is little written about this crucial topic. This primer discusses many areas where practitioners can enhance their assessment skills, including:

- Defining the assessment, including clarifying the referral question.
- Implications of recent research.
- Interviewing techniques.
- Factors to consider.
- Report writing.

This primer is hardly the final word on this topic. It is intended to provide guidelines, ideas, and a place to start. It is focused mostly on youth between the ages of twelve and seventeen, but may inform the assessment of younger children as well. While oriented towards males, it may be helpful to those working with females. Although professionals working with sexually abusive youth may disagree on many things, virtually all agree that assessment of youth requires extensive training and practice.

Some words on language are in order:

This book is written for professionals assessing youth who have sexually abused, and so this is the chosen term. These professionals may include probation officers and inpatient staff as well clinicians and administrators. It is applicable to formal (e.g., reports) as well as informal assessment (e.g., in-house incident reviews or treatment decisions). While most professionals who conduct formal assessments of youth are master's or doctoral level clinicians, assessment can occur at an informal level, as in the case of team discussions among law enforcement officials or staff in inpatient settings. This primer is intended to contain useful information for professionals of all backgrounds.

There is a strong trend away from the term "juvenile sex offender". In this primer it has been largely replaced with youth who have sexually abused. There are a number of reasons for this. First, it reflects our field's effort to label behaviors and not the person. Second, it serves to acknowledge that these young people are more than the sum of their harmful behaviors. Third, "sex offender" is, in its purest sense, a legal term. It is the abusive behavior that creates the offense, and therefore "offender" is not the most precise term. Finally, increased public awareness of the harm of sexual abuse by adults has resulted in the term "sex offender" taking on highly pejorative connotations that are not helpful to youth who are very much still in development. Although accurate language is important, the term "sex offender" can increase shame and act as a barrier to engagement in meaningful treatment.

This primer is written as an aid to others assessing the origins and possible trajectories of harmful sexual behavior by youth. Clearly, these issues overlap with other important aspects of young peoples' lives. Clinicians assessing these youth will also want to have a broad knowledge of adolescent development, sexuality, and co-occurring disorders. Professionals entering the field are sometimes confused by evidence of youthful sexuality and interest in sex; residential staff can struggle with where to set limits and how to define the line between acceptable and inappropriate self-expression. Likewise, it can be difficult for newer professionals to distinguish between features of adolescence such as moodiness and defiance and the symptoms of more serious disorders. Given the recent advances in understanding neurodevelopment (Siegel, 1999), it is all the more important that professionals stay within the bounds of their expertise and refer youth for additional assessments as needed.

Finally, it should be noted that there are, and should be, multiple perspectives on understanding youth. Different professionals can read the existing research and come to different conclusions regarding best practices, often with great fervor. Depending on the professional, examples might include the use of the polygraph or the best use of self-report measures. Much of this book draws upon the existing research, my own practical experience, and that of others willing to share their experiences. These are offered as possible resources, and not as the final word. What works for some professionals may not work for others. Readers are encouraged to seek out multiple resources for understanding this fascinating area of practice. A bibliography is included as Appendix B.

As with many other areas of human endeavor, starting with the basics is of fundamental importance.

What exactly is assessment?

Professionals frequently use the terms *evaluation* and *assessment* interchangeably, although their definitions sometimes differ across situation and jurisdiction. One commonly sees psychological assessments and evaluations containing similar referral questions, instruments, and types of recommendations. Given that language changes over time, it is entirely possible that there is so little difference between the two that no further consideration is necessary. However, as professionals strive to better understand youth, it may be wise to explore the meanings of each word in order to best define for themselves what it is they are asked to do, and what it is that they actually do. Professionals wanting to be more helpful may wish to focus first on the meanings of the most basic words that they use.

Webster's II New College Dictionary defines the word *evaluate* as "1. To determine or fix the value of. 2. To evaluate carefully: APPRAISE. 3. Math. To calculate or set down the numerical value of." The same dictionary defines *assessment* as "1. To estimate the value of property for taxation. 2. To set or determine the amount of (e.g., a tax or fine). 3. To charge (a person or property) with a special payment, as a tax or fine. 4. To appraise or evaluate." Webster (2001)

In what ways are these definitions different? One might notice that *evaluate* is based upon the word *value*, while *assess* often occurs in specific circumstances, such as property taxation. One can't assess property without assessing the context the property occurs in (e.g., city, rural, commercial, and residential). Each word is related to *appraise*, which Webster (2001) specifically defines as *"to determine the value of..."* and *"to estimate the worth or feature of..."* and yet one rarely sees documents related to juveniles with this word in the title, possibly due to its stricter definition or financial connotations.

For purposes of understanding juveniles, professionals might want to consider assessment as the gathering together of information in order to facilitate decisions. It may also be productive to think of assessment differently from evaluation in that the latter connotes numerical value. This becomes important when professionals ask themselves whether they are to consider information and make recommendations (e.g., "Given what is known about his intelligence, what interventions will be most useful") or whether they are to assign a value (e.g., "How intelligent is he?"). Both are important questions, yet without clarifying them, professionals may miss important information.

A different but equally important aspect is that assessment occurs in diverse situations (e.g., legal, school, and clinical settings) where full evaluations are not possible. Practitioners in inpatient settings such as residential treatment centers become involved in assessment processes each time they review an incident. A key question is whether they realize that they are involved in an assessment process, as this could inform what questions they ask of themselves and what resources they use. For example, having a simple framework for informal assessment of sexually abusive youth in critical incidents (such as disruptive behavior or rules violations) could provide more useful information than if the professional merely tries to manage the situation based on intuition or a reliance on past practice.

Assessment is flexible and diverse. It is common for people to engage in assessment without knowing it. From an evolutionary perspective, human beings are good at making rapid assessments in social situations and with respect to threat cues in the environment. We can be quite good at changing our assessments based on environmental data. For example, most new parents are quick to perceive new threats in their environment to keep their babies safe, and make adjustments such as covering electrical sockets and using car seats.

These latter examples involve assessment as an intuitive process without structure. This is where troubles can begin for professionals attempting to gather information and make decisions about a youth who has sexually abused. While a new parent's understanding of the world can help provide safety to their children, adherence to research and structured frameworks can help practitioners with youth make far better assessments. Meteorologists, for example, have made considerable strides in recent years by attending to scientific data as well as their own experience in understanding weather patterns. Those forecasting weather events, however, also have the benefit of a rather brief period between their assessments and feedback regarding their accuracy. This is certainly not the case in many aspects of assessment in sexually abusive youth, where assessors are often trying to gauge the likelihood of undesirable outcomes such as recidivism, treatment progress, or compliance with supervision; events that may only occur in the very long term.

Assessment is clearly a broad term, and there are as many ways to assess as there are situations to assess. Fundamental to our purposes is recognizing that the moment we are presented with a challenging situation such as understanding sexual abuse – which inherently thrives on secrecy – we become involved in assessment. To this end, professionals of all stripes will be at their best when they have a framework for understanding youth, and access to the best available information regarding the individual, their ecology, and the field of working with sexually abusive youth.

What kinds of assessments are most common?

Ultimately all assessments of youth who have sexually abused are done in order to help concerned others understand, whether at the present moment or at some time in the future. Some assessments are done for treatment planning, others for placement decisions (e.g., foster care or residential treatment, reunification in sibling incest situations), and still others to inform legal dispositions. The field of family assessment for sexually abusive youth remains underdeveloped.

The most controversial, most demanded, and least understood areas are risk and threat assessments. Risk assessments generally seek to answer the question, "What is the likelihood that this individual will engage in harmful sexual behavior (or violence, or other criminal behaviors) in the future?" Loosely defined, threat assessments seek to answer the question, "What is the likelihood of someone engaging in imminent harmful behaviors, and what immediate steps can be taken to prevent harm to others?" Research indicates that unguided clinical opinions are an ineffective means both for classification of individuals and for predicting which youth will abuse again. For example, Karl Hanson (2000) writes:

> "Predicting whether sexual offenders are going to recidivate is difficult. There is no shortage of studies in which expert evaluators failed to distinguish between low and high risk offenders (e.g., *Dix, 1976; Rice, Quinsey, & Harris, 1989; Sturgeon & Taylor, 1980*). The predictive accuracy of the typical clinical judgement is only slightly above chance levels (r = .10; *Hanson & Bussiere, 1998, p.1*)."

For this reason, practitioners should not undertake risk assessment without extensive training and review of the relevant literature. Even under these conditions, statements about risk should include strict time limitations on their findings. Prentky & Righthand (2003) recommend that their Juvenile Sex Offender Assessment Protocol – II be re-administered every six months. Further, this primer recommends not using the term "risk assessment" unless absolutely necessary. "*Risk assessment*" is certainly a common term in use from sexual abuser circles to financial sectors. In many, if not most cases, the over-arching question for our purposes is less "how risky is this youth" than "what needs to happen to reduce this young person's risk and keep him and others safe?" To this end, professionals may prefer to think in terms of *needs assessment*, to highlight areas in which adults can work to manage and reduce risk.

What kinds of methods are there?

Clinical assessments are made by a clinician, typically in the absence of objective measures. As noted above, unguided clinical risk assessments have not been supported in the literature. Purely clinical assessments can be highly subjective, difficult (if not impossible) to defend or challenge, and often take the form of an appeal to one's authority or experience ("based upon my twenty-two years of experience, I believe this young man to be among the most dangerous I have met"). Clinical risk assessments often rely upon information not supported by the literature (e.g., fire-setting).

Empirically guided assessment follows an established structure or protocol. A number of examples of empirically guided assessment methods are described in later sections. Advantages of empirically guided methods include their reliance on the research literature, their coverage of areas that unguided professionals might forget to consider, and their provision of common language across evaluators. Disadvantages can include their questionable psychometric properties (including inter-rater reliability) and questionable application to individual situations. Empirically guided methods often do not use research-based cutoff scores or provide discrete categories for decision-making. While the current empirically guided methods show promise, they require further study before they can be used in more than an exploratory fashion. They should not be used as a stand-alone guide to decision-making.

Actuarial assessment is, in its purest sense, an explicit and fixed method for arriving at a conclusion. For purposes of assessing sexual abusers, actuarial methods weigh specific factors and serve to compare an individual to one or more samples of others. Actuarial scales do not provide an absolute statement of an individual's likelihood for re-offense. A high score on a scale means that a sexual abuser's score is in the same range as a group of abusers whose known re-offense rate was at a specific percentage.

Actuarial scales can be very easy to use, are optimized for situations (such as sexual abuse) where recidivism can be unusual, and a number have been demonstrated to have moderate predictive validity. However, they are currently limited in their ability to provide other forms of information useful for applications to individuals (e.g., risk reduction strategies), and their contribution to understanding an individual can be quite limited.

Clinically adjusted actuarial assessment refers to using additional information to tailor one's estimate of risk for re-offense. For example, the lower-risk abuser who states an intention to re-offend is likely at higher risk than his actuarially derived score suggests. Individuals who display high levels of psychological factors whose relationship with sexual recidivism has been demonstrated may also be at higher risk than their scores suggest (Thornton, 2000, 2002).

What is the referral question?

This is the most important question professionals ask in an assessment. Properly understanding what others want to know is crucial to considering their questions. Many referral sources ask merely for an assessment. Consider the following:

Q: We need a risk assessment.

A: A risk assessment for what?

Q: For the kid. We need a solid report so we can know what to do.

A: About what?

Q: Our department is very concerned that he's going to get into trouble in the future.

A: What kind of trouble?

Q: Actually, that's a really good question. He's gotten in lots of trouble besides his sexual aggression, hasn't he?

A: Yes. Actually, the research is clear that sexually abusive youth are at greater risk to get into trouble for other kinds of crimes, like violence and property offenses.

Q: OK, but we're definitely concerned about his sexual behavior.

A: Fair enough, but what do you really want to know, and how do you really want to use this report?

Q: I guess we need something that tells us just how dangerous he is, and makes recommendations as to how we can best provide services.

A: What I hear you saying is you're looking for answers about how serious things could get in the future and what kinds of treatment and supervision would help to prevent his getting in trouble again?

Q: Yes. That's it.

A: How about this: I can provide a report that looks at who he is, how he came to abuse, what he and others need to do in the future so that it (hopefully) doesn't happen again. It can talk about what kinds of things professionals, family members, and the youth can look out for that would suggest he's on the road towards getting back in trouble.

Q: Perfect.

A: There's only one thing: this actually sounds like it's slanted more towards a needs assessment with recommendations than a risk assessment…

Q: My supervisor says we need a risk assessment.

A: There are no proven methods for accurate assessment of risk in young people. There are some good beginnings, but nothing that's been replicated or established through scientific rigor. It would likely be more accurate, and carry more weight if we call it either "an assessment of ongoing need" or a "needs assessment".

Q: OK, but my supervisor says we need a risk assessment. That's what convinces central office to follow the recommendations. They're very big on this.

A: I understand. If I call it a risk assessment, I will also have to include a section on how there are no empirically validated methods for classifying risk in young people. Ethically, I also have to include a statement to the effect that young people can change dramatically across adolescence, and that my assessment is therefore valid only for the coming months, the next year at the outside.

Q: Fair enough.

A: It sounds like this assessment is really intended to guide decisions around placement and treatment?

Q: Yes.

A: Then I'm also going to include a section on that, to make sure everyone knows that this is not a forensic evaluation for legal purposes. The purpose of this report is to assist professionals in helping this guy stay on track, and give some suggestions that will be useful to treatment providers. I'm going to make that explicit in the report. I know that any document can wind up in court, but I want to do what I can to prevent its use outside its intentions, OK? I just want to make sure about these things so I can be helpful to your agency, the kid, his family, and the community.

Q: Yes. You'd better do that. When can you start?

This is a simple discussion that does not occur often enough. The following questions may also be useful in constructing the most helpful assessments:

- When using the term "risk assessment", what exactly is the referral source asking for? A better understanding of the past? An explanation of a current offense? A prediction of the future? Assistance with case planning, treatment and supervision?

- What pressures exist to make recommendations in one way or another, and how do current circumstances influence those pressures (e.g., institutional, economic)?

- Given that much of an individual's development is not fully defined until adulthood, how can one best understand and communicate elements that may be important to treatment (e.g., remorse, empathy, personality traits)?

- How can one use the most accurate and precise language without pejorative jargon? Words such as "predator" may only serve to fuel the anxiety of the adults in the youth's life rather than inspire helpful interventions.

- How can one best create an environment where the youth will self report past behavior, attitudes, worries, and concerns?
- How can one best differentiate normative adolescent attitudes from those that support a re-offense process or signal an ongoing willingness to engage in harmful behavior?
- How can one recognize and describe empirically based indicators that signal escalation or imminence of harmful behavior?
- Does an assessment process gather information from all domains in the youth's life, such as his home, school, and community? (Prescott, 2006).

One critical aspect of assessment deserves mention: the factors that contribute to first offense are not necessarily those that contribute to re-offense. That is, while such aspects as family environment can contribute to a young person's sexual aggression, they do not necessarily drive a re-offense process. The willingness to engage in harmful sexual behavior and the willingness to persist despite detection, sanction, and treatment can be reasonably viewed as separate issues of concern.

Why be concerned?

Research demonstrates that juveniles commit 20 to 30% of reported rapes and 30 to 60% of child molestation (Hunter, 1999; Weinrott, 1996). Evidence exists that different trajectories of sexual aggression can signal different variations of risk in the short and long term (Hanson, 2000). However, it is important to note that typological studies of adolescents such as those reported by Hunter (2006) Knight and Prentky (1993) are still in their infancy.

Retrospective studies of adult pedophiles show that 40 to 50% report a juvenile onset to their offending. Same-sex pedophilia correlates with an earlier age of onset (Hunter, 1999). There is ample evidence that boy-victim adult pedophiles are at elevated risk for re-offense (e.g., Hanson & Bussiere, 1998; Hanson & Morton-Bourgon, 2004). While there is strong evidence that sexual interest and arousal is fluid and dynamic throughout adolescence (Hunter, 1999; Zolondek, Abel, Northey, & Jordan, 2001; Also see Nisbet, Wilson, & Smallbone, 2004; Prescott, 2006), it is clear that true offense-related sexual disorders can develop in youth.

Studies of juveniles who rape (e.g., Weinrott, 1996; Elliott, 1994) suggest that this form of sexual aggression is less likely to persist into adulthood. However, it is possible that these youth may be at an increased risk for general and violent recidivism (Worling & Curwen, 2000; Hanson & Bussiere, 1998). In some instances, sexual aggression may only be part of an emerging pattern of diverse criminality (Hare, 1991; Forth & Mailloux, 2000).

Finally, an understanding of base rates is essential to assessing risk (Serin & Brown, 2000; Webster, Ben-Aron, and Hucker, 1985; Monahan, 1981). However, gaining a sense of the overall base rate of adolescent sexual re-offense can be a frustrating experience. For example, Kenny, Keough, and Seidler (2001, p. 131) observe that "between 3% and 70% of first-time apprehended juvenile sex offenders reoffend." (Prescott, 2004).

The recidivism rates of sexually abusive youth have been studied across diverse jurisdictions. While many (e.g., Serin & Brown, 2000; Caldwell, 2002) have taken note of the importance of understanding base rates of re-offense, studies of adolescent sexual recidivism have been few and far between (Worling & Curwen, 2000). However, the available studies often find lower re-offense rates than one might expect. In one meta-analysis with 1,025 juveniles, Alexander (1999) found recidivism rates of 5.8% for rapists,

2.1% for child molesters, and 7.5% for "unspecified" adolescent abusers. While the length of follow-up varied across samples, she noticed that recidivism rates appeared to grow over time. Also of note, all were considered to have received abuse-specific treatment.

Langstrom and Grann (2000) found that among 46 adolescents aged 15 to 20, sexual recidivism was 20%, violent recidivism was 22%, and general recidivism (including violence) was 65% in a 6-year follow-up period. In contrast to Alexander's findings, the authors found that most of their recidivists did so within one to two years of follow-up. Caution is urged in interpreting these numbers. This sample represents nearly all of the young sexual offenders, ages 15-20, who received court-ordered forensic psychiatric evaluations in Sweden across a number of years. One can easily infer that, given the small size and apparently unusual circumstances of their selection, these must have been considered particularly problematic young people. Worling and Curwen (2000) followed 148 Canadian youth for an average of six years. They found that those who received "abuse specific" treatment had a 72% reduction in sexual recidivism. The untreated youth recidivated at 18% in the follow-up period, while the treated youth recidivated at a rate of 5%.

Clearly, all of these results must be interpreted with caution. First, ethical considerations have prevented the highest-quality randomized treatment/no-treatment comparisons. Even if these were possible, the specific "active ingredients" of treatment have yet to be determined, although Multisystemic Treatment (MST; Henggeler, Schoenwald, Borduin, Rowland, & Cunningham, 1998) appears especially promising. Second, recidivism rates are susceptible to adults' ability to detect re-offense. One may argue that these rates are grossly underestimated given that victims often do not report crimes. On the other hand, one might also argue that because youthful sexual abusers often have high rates of recidivism for nonsexual crimes, they are not particularly adept at evading detection. One might further argue that upon arrest for sexually abusive behavior, many youth have far less opportunities for re-offense due to increased supervision.

In summary, when we undertake the assessment of sexually abusive youth, we must understand that it is statistically most likely that they will next come into contact with the legal system for some other kind of crime. Some studies (e.g., Langstrom & Grann, 2000) find rates of violent re-offense only slightly higher than sexual re-offense. The youthful sexual recidivist is unusual in American studies. Because of the diversity of problematic outcomes, it might be most useful to frame assessments as how adults can best help youth become responsible adults.

What principles are involved?

Before moving into the specifics of assessment, it may be useful to review some of the basic principles underlying assessment:

> Andrews and Bonta (2003) describe three principles in understanding criminal offenders: *risk, need,* and *responsivity*. The *risk principle* states that interventions should be matched to the risk the offender poses. The *need principle* states that interventions should specifically target areas related to criminal behavior, and the *responsivity principle* states that interventions should match the characteristics of the offender. These distinctions are critical to accurate assessment. It is simple for the novice to equate treatment needs with level of risk. A low-risk youth who has difficulty responding to treatment that is poorly matched to his needs and abilities might appear more worrisome to those around him, and therefore at higher risk than he really is. For example, a low-functioning incest abuser who is non-compliant with treatment targeting sexual deviance may appear more problematic than he is. Assuming that he is truly low risk (e.g., no prior history of sexual aggression, no attitudes tolerant of sexual abuse, etc.), these interventions may be less effective than education and restorative treatment tailored to his abilities and targeting interpersonal deficits. In this case, an assessment of *risk, need,* and *responsivity* would be more

helpful to others than simply making a statement
about "high risk" or "low risk". (Prescott, 2006)

In this view, "risk" is essentially an underlying predisposition,
akin to a psychological trait, related to the willingness to abuse
others despite factors that would deter others. This kind of willingness is nearly impossible to view directly, except in occasional
statements and threats (e.g., "I'll do it again"). Even the actuarial
scales in existence only employ "markers" or "proxies" for risk,
such as number of prior convictions and other historical factors
fixed in an individual's history.

In this author's review of the literature, research has identified
only a few indicators of risk in young people. These include:

- Early onset refers to a pattern of behavior and not just the
  fact that a pre-pubertal individual engaged in harmful
  sexual behavior. Typically, the available research uses the
  age of twelve as a cutoff point in determining early onset.

- Persistence refers to harmful sexual behavior persisting
  despite detection, despite sanction, and despite treatment.
  Persistence is not the same thing as having numerous victims before the first instance of detection (Worling, 2004;
  Thornton, 2002). Useful questions include to what extent
  has this behavior persisted and under what circumstances? The youth who persists despite family awareness,
  arrest, involvement with the legal system, and while
  under the supervision of staff in a residential treatment
  center may well represent a greater cause for concern than
  the young person who persists despite parental admoni-
  tion.

- Clearly established deviant sexual preferences. Central to
  this is that youth must show a clear preference for behavior that is likely to bring them into contact with the law
  (cf. Hanson & Bussiere, 1998). However, proper explo-
  ration is critical. What may appear to be a clearly established pattern among youth, particularly younger adolescents, can change (Nisbet, Wilson, & Smallbone, 2004;

Epperson, Ralston, Fowers, DeWitt, & Gore, 2006). For example, take the case of a young man who steals underwear from his neighbor's clothesline. What is the most problematic aspect of this behavior? Is it that he masturbated with the underwear? If so, this is not entirely uncommon among young men. Is it that he stole the underwear? If so, this may be more related to a willingness to engage in generally illegal behavior than illegal sexual behavior. Is the greatest concern that he prefers masturbating with the underwear to seeking out appropriate peer-age relationships? This could indicate a sexual behavior problem, although it is important to recall that the sexual arousal patterns of youth are more subject to change than those of their adult counterparts. Many, if not most, youth will find their interests move from the underwear to the underwear's owner by the time they reach maturity. Very often youth are willing to self disclose these kinds of interests.

With respect to sexual re-offense, it may be useful to think in terms of the following domains:

- Offense-related sexual deviance.
- Contributory attitudes (permission-giving self-statements that support sexual aggression).
- Interpersonal/socio-affective functioning.
- Self-management (e.g., problem-solving, impulsivity).
- Significant others (that support sexual aggression, whether implicitly or explicitly).

These domains are explored later in this primer.[1]

The responsivity principle further requires that professionals understand the characteristics (personal, familial, cultural) of the abuser and match services accordingly. Individuals will respond differently to different types and styles of interventions. While developmentally delayed individuals will clearly not benefit from treatment designed for and implemented with higher functioning individuals, other factors such as learning disabilities and co-occurring psychiatric conditions should also be taken into account.

Ward, Day, Howells, and Birgden (2004) have added to these principles the idea of "readiness". They write:

> We argue that there has been little attempt in the literature to distinguish between three distinct, although related, constructs: treatment motivation, responsivity, and readiness. Motivation involves assessing whether or not someone really wants to enter treatment and therefore is willing to change his or her behavior in some respect (e.g., cease to behave aggressively). Typical clinical criteria for deciding that offenders are motivated to enter treatment include expressions of regret for their offenses, a desire to change, and sounding enthusiastic about the treatments available. In one important respect, the judgment that an offender is motivated for therapy is essentially a prediction that he or she will engage in, and complete, therapy. In current practice, it is widely accepted that offender motivation constitutes an important requirement for selection into rehabilitation programs, and therapists are expected to have the skills to initiate, enhance, and sustain motivation in reluctant individuals. Ironically, despite a plethora of literature on motivational interviewing and related interventions, there has been comparatively little attention paid to clarifying the relevant underlying mechanisms or consideration of the relationship between motivational states and other aspects of treatment preparedness. (p. 646)

The authors go on to distinguish between internal and external readiness, and provide simple ideas for motivating the "low-

[1] For further information on these domains, see Thornton (2002), and Ward & Beech (2004).

readiness" client. These are useful because they can help professionals consider how best to communicate an understanding of the young person:

- Internal Readiness:
    1. Cognitive
    2. Affective
    3. Behavioral
    4. Volitional
    5. Personal identity
- External Readiness:
    1. Circumstance
    2. Location
    3. Opportunity
    4. Resource
    5. Support (including family and extended family)
    6. Program/Timing
- Motivation of low readiness:
    1. Modify the client
    2. Modify the therapy
    3. Modify the setting

Useful areas to consider when addressing readiness include guilt and shame. Each can inform an understanding of a young person's confidence, motivation, and internal readiness for change. Tangney and Dearing (2002) have found that:

> In brief, shame is an extremely painful and ugly feeling that has a negative impact on interpersonal behavior. Shame-prone individuals appear relatively more likely to blame others (as well as themselves) for negative events, more prone to a seething, bitter, resentful kind of anger and hostility, and less able to empathize with others in general. Guilt, on the other hand, may not be that bad after all. Guilt-prone individuals appear better able to empathize with others and to accept responsibility for

negative interpersonal events. They are relatively less prone to anger than their shame-prone peers – but when angry, these individuals appear more likely to express their anger in a fairly direct (and one might speculate, more constructive) manner. This is an intriguing pattern, and it is the aspect of shame and guilt that has the most direct applied implications – for parents, teachers, and clinicians alike.

In summary, key questions include:

What is known about this person's underlying willingness to continue their involvement in harmful behaviors?

What kinds of treatment needs might they have that relate to engaging in harmful or illegal behaviors?

What psychological factors should treatment providers and supervisory adults know about in order to best meet this young person's needs?

What kinds of risk factors are there?

Assessments that guide treatment planning, placement, and supervision strategies will focus on diverse areas of the youth's functioning. Risk factors, or those elements that signal an underlying propensity to persist in harmful sexual behavior, have been difficult for researchers to isolate.

The classification of risk factors into *static* (those elements solidly fixed in a person's history, such as gender, or number of convictions) and *dynamic* (elements that are subject to change) has gained appeal in recent years (Ryan, 2005). Of the dynamic variables, Hanson (2000) has differentiated between those that remain relatively *stable* across time, such as personality disorder or self-regulation style, and those that are *acute*, and subject to rapid change or escalation. Examples of acute factors include substance abuse, anger, or other negative moods. These distinctions are important. Hanson and Bussiere (1998) found that substance abuse did not distinguish recidivists from non-recidivists in long-term studies of adult sex offenders, while Hanson and Harris (2001) found it to be a useful indicator of imminence.

Adult actuarial scales have succeeded largely due to the static nature of their variables, particularly their reliance on past behavior. This has been apparent in the predictive validity of scales such as the VRAG (Quinsey, Harris, Rice, & Cormier, 1998), Static 99 (Hanson & Thornton, 2000), and Rapid Risk Assessment of Sex Offender Recidivism (RRASOR; Hanson, 1997). However, many researchers recognize the problems involved in predicting future events. Williams (1975) reported on a study of differences in men serving their first sentences in the British prison system, and those who had previously been imprisoned. While only one in three of the first sentence offenders were re-convicted, two thirds of the recidivists were re-convicted again. Although the researchers looked at 40 variables among the prisoners, they concluded: "the major difference between individuals in prison is those serving their first sentence and the rest" (p. 36).

Hanson and Bussiere (1998) found that typical clinical judgment yielded an average correlation not much better than chance (r= .10) while prior convictions on their own correlated at .20. Likewise, in their review of the Hare Psychopathy Checklist: Screening Version (PCL: SV; Hart, Cox, & Hare, 1995), Monahan and his colleagues (2001) found that although PCL: SV scores were the strongest predictor of violence in their sample, the items specifically related to past behavior were the most predictive. Of note, the Hare psychopathy scales were developed to measure a construct ("psychopathy") commonly associated with persistent criminality and not the likelihood of future criminality itself. More recently, Marczyk, Heilbrun, Lander, and DeMatteo (2003) noted that the most predictive aspects of several scales were not their total scores, but the subscales related to past behavior, suicidal thoughts, anger, fighting, and anxiety. The scales measured included the Psychopathy Checklist: Youth Version (PCL: YV; Forth, Kosson, & Hare, 2003) and Youth Level of Service/Case

Management Inventory (YLS/CMI; Hoge & Andrews, 2003). Of interest to practitioners, the authors found that the referring offenses that brought youth to the attention of the authorities were not in themselves predictive. They concluded that the use of these tools for prediction "may not be a straightforward process" (p. 15).

Further complicating matters, some authors have observed that including too much information in the decision-making process can result in reduced accuracy of assessments (Monahan, 1981, p. 88; Quinsey, 2000). Quinsey, Harris, Rice, & Cormier (1998) observe that "More importantly, the amount of information available to the clinician was unrelated to accuracy but was highly related to the degree of confidence in the judgment", and that humans "are, in fact, most confident when making extreme judgments" (p. 56).

Reviewing the role of past behavior in understanding adults, two observations can be made. First, as Zamble and Quinsey (1997) observed, static variables ultimately reflect dynamic processes. One recidivates as a result of a persistent willingness to do so, and not simply because of their number of prior convictions. Past behavior may signal persistence, but it is not necessarily the same thing. Second, many adolescents who persist in harming others well into adulthood simply do not have the time to accrue the kinds of risk markers that have made the adult actuarial measures robust. One might wonder if it is not the persistence of risk factors into adulthood that accounts for the recent successes of these tools.

Finally, one may question the role of dynamic risk factors when youth itself is dynamic. In their most recent version of the Juvenile Sex Offender Assessment Protocol (JSOAP – II), Prentky and Righthand (2003) observe that "No aspect of their development, including their cognitive development, is fixed or stable. In a very real sense, we are trying to assess the risk of 'moving targets'." For this reason, they recommend that youth be re-assessed every six months (p. i).

In a recent review of the general recidivism literature regarding juveniles, Quinsey and his colleagues (2004) note that the best predictors of juvenile delinquency among youth in the general population, ages six through eleven, are a prior history of offending, substance abuse, gender, low socioeconomic status, and having an antisocial parent. The best predictors for young people ages 12-14 are a lack of strong prosocial ties, antisocial peers, and prior delinquent offenses (p. 91). They observe that "Theories to account for the patterns of these markers tend to focus on narrow domains. In the absence of a more general theory, the wealth of correlates of antisocial behavior that are themselves intercorrelated is something of an encumbrance rather than a benefit." The authors describe three types of adolescent antisociality: "adolescence-limited delinquents, … early-starting life-course-persistent antisocial individuals whose behaviors are associated with neuropathology resulting from prenatal, perinatal, and/or postnatal problems, sometimes in combination with family and neighborhood adversity", and "early-starting life-course-persistent antisocial individuals" without neurodevelopmental pathology. They note that this third category appears to comprise a distinct class of individual, or taxon, different from other antisocial individuals (p. 94).

A dynamic factor that is less understood is treatment failure. Hanson and Bussiere (1998) found that failure of adults to complete treatment contributed to risk in the absence of other factors. Similarly, Hunter and Figueredo (1999) found that youth who were unable to complete treatment had higher levels of sexual maladjustment, suggesting elevated long-term risk.

Perhaps just as important as *risk* factors, is an understanding of *protective factors* (Bremer, 1998, 2001, 2006a; Gilgun, 2006). Bremer (2006b) defines protective factors as the building blocks of resilience, while Gilgun (2006) describes resilience as involving the resources that help young people cope with, adapt to, and overcome risk (p. 383). Beyond their practical utility in understanding a young person, understanding reliance (and the factors that contribute to it) can help guide the efforts of treatment providers, families, and other concerned adults. After all, the resources that a youth brings with them to the process of change will likely remain in the young person's life long after the treatment providers are gone. Interventions that enhance resilience have the potential to help young people across their lives.

What are some do's and don'ts for getting started on assessment?

1) Ensure that you have all the proper consent forms, releases, and waivers of confidentiality. Although this could be the topic of an entire volume, it suffices to say that this kind of preparation is key. The parties involved have a right to know where your report is going and how it will be shared. They should be very clear as to the purpose of your report, the inherent risks and benefits, and the limits of your confidentiality. To this end, you may wish to consult with other professionals and your attorney to ensure that you are properly prepared to undertake these specialized assessments.

2) Conducting a thorough file review is among the most important elements. This can include:
- Police reports.
- Psychological evaluation reports.
- Previous psychosexual reports.
- Victim impact statements or official accounts of the offense.
- Relevant school reports (regarding progress, behavior, or learning disabilities).
- Protective service records.
- Other records of delinquency.

In starting an assessment, professionals should acquaint themselves with all pertinent records, including psychological and educational evaluations (IQ, learning disabilities, emotional disturbances, etc.) and take note of past diagnoses, as they can reflect both the youth's experiences and how others have experienced the youth. Assessors should ensure that they have complete file information and make it clear that holding back records could compromise the assessment. There are several reasons for this:

- Multiple perspectives can be extremely useful. Who speaks highly or disparagingly of this young person and why? In what domains does one find the most difficulty? Their home? Their school? Their functioning in the community?

- Diagnoses can change across time and vary according to the purpose of the review. A prior sexual abuse evaluation may not address psychiatric co-morbidity, while previous school assessments may overlook psychological conditions. All should be considered to properly understand the individual.

- Historical information can be erroneous or distorted through previous file review. Like the youth they serve, professionals can make mistakes and be unreliable historians. Also, original reports can often provide information that subsequent synopses don't.

- Likewise, professionals asked to provide a formal assessment of a young person with whom they work might be tempted to skip a thorough file review with the belief that they already know the case thoroughly. This is a common and easily avoidable mistake.

- Finally, some youthful sexual abusers, and even their families, just might lie. While this has been the source of a number of cruel and unprofessional jokes, the fact remains that professionals are not always able to create an environment in which youth and their families are willing to completely disclose aspects of their most shameful and regrettable experiences.

3) Ensure that your assessment environment is conducive to building trust, gaining honesty, and encouraging self-disclosure. This includes both office space and interpersonal style. It is useful to remember that many youthful sexual abusers have themselves been victimized, traumatized, and neglected. Although their

harmful behaviors can be horrific, it does not help a comprehensive assessment to appear punitive, impatient, or demanding. Further, by coming into an assessment, the youth is likely already aware that they are about to have a challenging experience. While this can be useful, it is easy for adults to be viewed as punitive.

4) Anticipate resistance and consider it a normal part of the assessment and treatment experience. Even the most normal adolescents may appear aloof and unwilling to share personal information. It is easy to lose sight of the fact that it is difficult for most well adjusted adults to be completely open and honest, particularly with respect to private details related to embarrassing material. In some cases, sexually abusive youth feel that a fundamental fairness is lacking when they were caught while others who have harmed them were not.

5) Expect objections, for the reasons mentioned above. Before entering an interview, it helps to be psychologically prepared for objections, resistance, denial, and the other actions that people use to avoid accepting responsibility and engaging in heartfelt dialogue. Be aware that objections often reflect a pro-social orientation, and can be used accordingly to "disarm" the objection. For example:

> Young person: I would never do something like that! My mom and dad would never let me live it down!

> Adult: Yes, I can see that you're the kind of person who values his relationship with his parents. What would it be like if you could talk about your mistakes with them?

> YP: I might have done something, but not what she said. She's all confused.

> A: I know it's easy to get confused. What do you think would help you get through this?

6) Don't believe that denial of sexual aggression *necessarily* means that the youth is likely to abuse again. Although it is true that some individuals are falsely accused of sexual aggression, this section will assume that the individual's culpability has been estab-

lished. For many years those working with sexual abusers assumed that denial is related to sexual re-offense risk. However, recent meta-analyses (Hanson & Morton-Bourgon, 2004) found no correlation between denial and risk. There are many views on how this may be. They include:

- Perhaps researchers are measuring denial differently than practitioners.

- Perhaps denial is more closely related to readiness and motivation for treatment, or to the responsivity principle. Perhaps its connection to re-offense is not as direct and "washes out" of research findings.

- Perhaps denial simply indicates that the person is not ready to admit what they've done.

One may reasonably ask how a person can engage in treatment for sexual aggression if they are not willing to admit the problem. Some practitioners believe that it is possible to engage in treatment that reduces the willingness to engage in harmful behaviors in general, including sexual aggression. Others may be willing to engage in abuse-specific treatment without fully divulging the extent of their abuse history.

Ultimately, we know:

- Denial has not been found to be related to sexual recidivism among sex offenders.

- Many individuals simply do not want to acknowledge high-stakes behaviors such as sexual aggression.

- Many individuals take longer than others to fully disclose their actions in assessment and treatment situations.

It helps to recognize that denial may simply indicate that we have not done our job right yet. It may be that many things drive a re-offense process, but that just because a young person denies his actions does not mean he will do it again.

7) Do not believe that an apparent lack of empathy and remorse *necessarily* means that the youth is likely to abuse again. This, too, has been a widely held belief for many years. It is also common for news media items to capitalize on a young person's apparent lack of remorse.

Two things are important:

- As with denial, there is no research evidence linking empathy and remorse with sexual re-offense.
- Youth are at very different developmental stages than their adult counterparts.

Those interested in empathy will wish to review the extensive literature in this area (e.g., Fernandez, 2002). Those interested in remorse will note that although it is included in the Hare Psychopathy Checklist – Youth Version (Forth, Kosson, & Hare, 2003), a scale found to have applications to risk assessment, it is only predictive when combined with other factors.

What about the victims?

It is easy for professionals to focus exclusively on the youth, their risk factors, and their management to the exclusion of those impacted by sexual abuse: the families and the victims. The safety, location, and well being of sexual abuse victims should always be taken into consideration. Providing victim-centered services is a well established field in itself, and professionals are urged to familiarize themselves with it in order to serve their clients and communities the most effectively.

Hindman (2005) has advocated adopting a stance that "victims are watching". This can be a useful strategy for the assessor to keep in mind when framing recommendations. Collaboration with others who have assessed the victim can be crucial to the well being of abuser and survivor alike. It can be easier to make recommendations for treatment that reduces recidivism risk than treatment that also focuses on providing restitution to victims.

Interviewing sexually abusive youth

The clinical interview is where the assessment of sexually abusive youth becomes as much art as science. Early writing on the topic emphasized the need for interviews to take charge and control the interview. Gray and Wallace (1992) suggest that interviewers "use silence for power in the interview, it can help build client anxiety". While these recommendations occur with the recognition that they need to behave respectfully, they have sometimes been used as a license to engage in interviewing techniques that more closely resemble interrogation. Professionals will do best to understand the differences between interview and interrogation.

Recent research has demonstrated that therapists whose style might be described as warm, empathic, rewarding, and directive (sometimes known by the acronym WERD) are able to produce better treatment outcomes than those whose style is harsh and confrontational (Marshall, Fernandez, Serran, Mulloy, Thornton, Mann, & Anderson, 2003). Motivational enhancement techniques have also become better established and widely accepted (e.g., Miller & Rollnick, 2002).

Professionals can never be entirely sure what will unfold during an interview, so it is recommended that the location of the interview be carefully prepared to ensure the safety of youth and adult alike. Ensure that you are each comfortable. It helps to ensure that while the location is private, it is not so isolated that you could not get help on short notice. Isolation from others can also result in the youth experiencing a lack of safety that might result in unnecessary (and avoidable) resistance.

Professionals should expect to be in charge of the interview, but this need not equate to being demanding or pushy. Preparing a semi-structured list of questions can assure that the interviewer stays focused on key issues while allowing the youth to influence the direction of the interview. Trying too hard to control the interview may exclude information that the youth brings to the table, whether directly, indirectly, or by accident. Many interviewers have tried to clarify one important issue only to have other very important issues surface. Ultimately it is the task of the professional to collect this necessary data in a way that ensures the comfort and disclosure of the youth. One can always return to the key issues as needed. To this end, a written list of key issues can be invaluable. Proper preparation for an interview involves:

1. *Consent forms and confidentiality waivers.* This ensures that all parties understand what is happening.

2. *A thorough file review.* In other disciplines it may be advisable to meet the client first and review the file thoroughly later. This is a mistake. It is very easy to unknowingly miss important information, only to have to go back and seek it out later.

3. *Office safety.* A sense of safety for both parties contributes to a more productive interview and prevents tragedy.

4. *Prepare key questions.* The file review will contain areas for clarification and further inquiry. A written list will keep the interview grounded, and the interviewer more confident and comfortable.

Anxiety and fear

In trying to create an environment where a youth may self report his behaviors and attitudes, it becomes apparent that an interview for assessing sexual aggression is inherently anxiety provoking. Anxiety appears in all human relationships at various times and in varying degrees. The professional attempting to obtain information about difficult material may simply want to recognize this fact. One can influence the ebb and flow of anxiety through silence, language, and body posture. At some points in an interview it may be necessary to increase or decrease anxiety in order to meet both the short-term needs of the interview and the long-term needs of the youth. As the professional considers how much they want to control this ebb and flow of anxiety, it may be best to remember the axiom of "do no harm". Many interviewers have felt that the most important aspect of an interview is to "break down denial" regarding the referral offense. This need not be the case, and it can easily become counterproductive when it hinders the flow of related information, including insights into the beliefs and attitudes of the young person. Anxiety is a natural part of an interview. Introducing fear can be counterproductive and even harmful. Angry and fearful people rarely listen very well, and rarely say what they really mean.

Interviewing tips

1) Begin with an extensive introduction. This accomplishes two things:

First, this can ease the mind of the young person who is understandably anxious about having to share details around shameful events. Often an interviewer may inject thoughts and values into a conversation that influence the tone of the interview. Such statements as "I've worked with kids a long time, and I know about the courage and honor it takes to be able to talk openly and honestly" can set the stage for disclosure later on. In order to build a working rapport, it may reduce anxiety to explain the assessment process in great detail. This includes explaining what it is like to be assessed and providing assurances that they will be all right when it's over. Your "script" might read something like this:

> *I've worked with many young people like you who are struggling with becoming the person they want to be. This assessment is going to focus on some things that are hard to talk about, but that you can talk about. I'm going to ask some questions, and you might notice that we jump around topics a bit, but when we do, I'm going to bring it back to the things we need to talk about. At the end, we're going to make sure that everything's going OK and that we have a plan to make sure you get on with your business in one piece and feeling as safe as you can be. I know you have a lot going on for you right now. Can you handle this?*

Second, it can prepare the young person to tell the truth:

> *Other people are concerned about the behaviors that led to your arrest. Part of my job is to determine how honest you are with me, and this is something I've done for many years. While it might have been in your best interest to admit as little as possible in the criminal justice system, full admission in treatment goes along with better treatment, more trust, and less trouble with the legal system. Other people besides me make decisions about punishment. This evaluation and its con- clusions, recommendations, etc. will be considered by others in making decisions about your placement, treatment, discharge, etc. I have to tell the truth, and I am going to tell the truth – to you and to others. If I don't feel you're being honest, I am going to have to say so. When you're honest, I will absolutely report that as well. I don't say this to be threatening; I just want us to be clear. You deserve to know where I'm coming from and so I'm telling you honestly and directly.*

Note the positive assumption that the youth will comply. *"When you tell the truth…"* produces a distinctly different response than *"Don't you lie to me"*. It can also be useful to convey requirements in a fashion that does not appear coercive. For example:

- "You need to" can be replaced with "please" ("please be respectful" as opposed to "you need to stop swearing").
- "You will" or "you better" can be replaced with "I expect you to" ("I expect you to be honest" can produce a different response than "you better be honest")

In the end, a carefully prepared introduction can illustrate the axiom that *"the slower you go, the faster you get where you want to be"*.

2) When seeking out factual information, *always* start with highly open-ended questions. For example:

Q: Please tell me everything that happened that day.

A: Why? (Note the attempt to understand the question to begin the process of self editing)

Q: Because that will help me understand. Please tell me everything that happened that day. (A faint, encouraging smile can help. Asking the question again can prevent a divergent tactic such as "Why do you have to know?)

A: Where do you want me to start? (In other words "I can tell you what you want to hear if you'll tell me how to do it.)

Q: From the beginning (encouraging smile).

A: Do you mean from when I got up or when I got into trouble, or…

Q: Wherever you like (shrug and encouraging smile).

A: But that's a lot of… can't you just ask me…

Q: I can ask you more specific questions when you tell me everything that happened that day[2].

This may be an extreme example, but it illustrates an important point. Most youth are motivated to disclose only what they have to disclose. Keeping questions open invites all information into the interview. This information might include aspects that future treatment providers will be grateful to know, or it could be a window into the life of the young person, including his thoughts, attitudes, or relationships. From a clinical standpoint, the youth will likely start at a point of considerable relevance.

A helpful metaphor might be that of a painter who only has a blank canvas at the very beginning of his work. Once he starts to paint, he commits himself to the process. Similarly, once a young person starts to tell his story the interview can unfold. It is often easier to ask clarifying questions than to try to work backwards to find new information in an older story.

Open-ended questions may invite a long-winded and wandering response. These can always be directed back to the events of the day in question.

---

[2] Much of this question and answer sequence is explored further by Avinoam Sapir. For more information see www.Lsiscan.com.

3) Ask questions that make positive assumptions. Sometimes it can help to grossly overestimate the number of times they have been involved in sexual aggression in order for them to feel more comfortable providing an accurate answer. For example, asking the question "did you have sex with him more than five times" is easy to deny. Framing the question as "I imagine you did this kind of thing at least 500 times" can make a young person respond with a higher number than in the first example. Obviously, youth can be vulnerable to the effects of adults around them, and some suggestible youth may use this as an opportunity to over-report their activities in the hopes of pleasing the interviewer. Care should be taken to tailor all questions to the needs and abilities of the youth.

4) Be aware of nonverbal language. It is not always a good indicator of deception, but it can be a very helpful indicator of anxiety and attitude:

- Is the youth leaning in the direction of the door?
- Does he take off his coat or leave it zipped all the way up?
- Does he exhibit anxiety through pressured speech or jiggling his leg (which one youth referred to as "the magic knee")?
- Does he appear to enjoy the recounting of harmful sexual behavior?
- Does his nervousness increase or decrease during the course of the interview?
- Do his eyes become glazed at any point (possibly signaling a level of dissociation)?
- Do his pupils dilate at any point (possibly signaling an arousal state)?
- Does the youth keep his arms crossed?
- Does he pick up items or try to take the interviewer's seat?
- Does he sit in such a way that his groin area is highlighted?
- Does he appear sexually aroused by the conversation?
- Does he engage in nervous or self-harmful behaviors such as picking at scabs, fingernails, etc.?

5) Be aware of omissive or evasive responses. Most deception is not accomplished by telling lies, but by distracting the person being deceived by leaving out key information or drawing attention away from it:

- What the heck would I do that for?
- Who said I did that?
- They don't know what they're talking about; they're nuts, etc.
- Are you accusing me of…
- That's a hard question! I… uh…
- Are you asking me… (Repeating the question stalls for time to concoct an answer.)
- I would never do something like that.
- Why can't you people quit with this already?
- I told you all a thousand times…

Another familiar indicator of extensive youthful self-editing is when a story seems to jump from one direction to another:

"What happened was… you see… she and I… I went out with my friends, and then later on…"

6) Maintain clear and ethical boundaries.

- Never agree to keep secrets.
- Never express a belief that the young person will not harm others again.
- Avoid power struggles and remain neutral.
- Do not abuse the client, either physically, sexually, psychologically, or through shame.
- Keep personal disclosure limited to routine, simple, or casual aspects: "I like the Red Sox" is OK; "I have a cousin who tried out for the Red Sox" is not. There is generally no good reason to share personal information and many reasons not to. However, exchanges around sports, music, monster-cars, and other matters of interest to young people can help break the ice in an interview. A guiding principle is that the profes-

sional who interviews sexually abusive youth will always occupy that role in the youth's mind, and any change of roles, especially towards a more personal relationship can cause confusion and harm. Professionals will wish to consult the ethics of their various professions where questions arise.

- Be sure to engage in supervision and consultation to meet the long-term needs of young people. If need be, engage in therapy to address the impact of working with this population.

General interviewing strategies

The following suggestions are based on the work of Lambie and Robson (2006). They are useful for those assessing young people with whom one may come into contact in other professional situations (e.g., within an inpatient setting). They serve as reminders of general interviewing techniques that can encourage honesty even in difficult situations such as initial assessments of sexually abusive youth:

It's about relationships. Putting the client at ease increases the likelihood of honesty in counseling. Professionals often notice that youth seem to need to talk about everything other than the reason they are there. The aim of an assessment interview is honesty, not compliance. The professional should state from the beginning that they have experience with other adolescents who have sexually abused and will not be shocked by what they might be told. This establishes credibility and control of the interview. Statements like these can be helpful:

- *Its tough being here having to talk to grown ups about what you've done.*
- *Lots of boys like you feel so much shame and embarrassment that it's hard to talk honestly.*
- *Sometimes it's easier to get it off your chest all at once.*
- *It will get easier to talk more about your actions the more you get to know me and the more times you meet me.*
- *Many of the other guys that I talk to describe how pleased they are*

when they have talked about it all. Its like they've taken a huge load off their shoulders.

The professional will seem especially credible if they can predict what the adolescent might be thinking and the extent of their behavior.

Treat others as you would like to be treated. This means both verbal and non-verbal behavior. The professional should create a context for respectful behavior in the interview and model this for the adolescent. Only respectful sexually explicit language should be allowed (no sexually aggressive terms for body parts, etc.). While there is a time and a place for permitting provocative language as youth express themselves, professionals need to be on guard against behavior deterioration or allowing abusiveness to become a part of the interview process. In some cases, setting limits on language can provide an unspoken sense of safety to youth.

Talk with (not down to) young people. If challenging the adolescent's cognitive distortions, the clinician could say "I respect you and believe you deserve a better life than that of abusing others, so I want to be really honest with you about your abuse." This way the professional models respect and honesty. Although sexual aggression touches off strong emotions in all, the professional should take care not to distance the adolescent by showing strong emotional reaction to their disclosures and take any issues that need to be processed to supervision.

Professionals should be aware of the importance of not just under-disclosing, but also over-disclosing their sexual misconduct. Young people may want to please professionals and tell them what they think the professional wants to hear. This can be particularly true of younger children and those who are intellectually disabled. "More" does not necessary equal a more honest disclosure, nor a better one! The professional should support and praise disclosures made by the young person for being honest as this increases the likelihood that they will be more honest in the future.

Use simple language. This helps young people talk about their offending in as much detail as possible, and allows them sufficient time. While we may understand what we are saying, the young person may have no idea. The professional's goal should be to use language that is even more straightforward than they feel the young person needs to understand. Adolescents often have little respect for people who patronize them and use long words that go over their heads.

Embarrassment and shame are part of the game. We have all done things we are ashamed of and embarrassed about. Looking back on these experiences it is common to feel some shame; such feelings are normal. It is important to support the young person without condoning their abusive behavior. Talking about it might be hard, but it's also the beginning of becoming a healthier person. Acknowledging that there is more they can and should talk about is usually realistic and often sets the stage for later treatment. This sends a message that is understandable if they later make a more honest disclosure of what happened. It is also common for adolescents to remember more details of their abusing the more they talk about it. The more they are able to do this, the more adults can help them do no further harm. Professionals can expect cognitive distortions and it is helpful to remember the motivational interviewing slogan of "rolling with resistance" when faced with clear denial and minimization of offending.

Useful Interview Questions

The following is not so much an interview schedule, but a list of useful questions:

- Why would someone do this?
- Under what circumstances would someone do this?
- How do you feel being asked about this?
- Why do you think others are concerned you did this?
- Did you tell any family members about this situation? (Why not?)

- Who would have had the opportunity to do this?
- Have you ever thought of doing something like this even though you didn't follow through on those thoughts?
- Why wouldn't you do this?
- What do you think should happen to the person who did this?
- Do you think the person who did this deserves a second chance?
- Under what conditions would they deserve a second chance?
- Has anyone been affected by your sexual behavior? If so, Who? In what ways?
- Even though you knew what you were doing was wrong, what were you telling yourself that made it seem OK to...
- Although you're not allowed to talk to ___ right now, what would you say to ___ if s/he were here right now?
- With everything you've told me, what would it take for you to...
- What do you think is the most unacceptable element of this offense?
- Tell me about other people you've touched sexually.
- By the time someone gets arrested for ___, they've usually done it lots of times. I imagine you've done this at least ___ times? And you've also ___?
- Kids sometimes find others saying they don't want to have sex but acting like they do, so they just have sex with that person anyway. Please tell me about times you've done that.

Dynamic Risk Factors

Dynamic factors, or those areas of functioning that can change over time, are critical to understand in order to construct effective treatment and intervention strategies. As noted earlier, many of the elements apparent in an interview (e.g., denial, remorse, empathy) have turned out to have little contribution to risk, but can provide information about motivation and readiness for treatment. Evidence of dynamic risk, however, can seem to flourish in front of one's eyes in a clinical interview, while evidence of the same factors may be lacking in the file. The same times when interviewers are observing denial and the absence of guilt or remorse can be those that provide the most information about dynamic factors. The following framework will assist professionals with their formulations and those at the front lines to understand situations as they unfold. Rather than being a simple list, these factors may interact with each other and provide insight into "implicit theories" that the young person has about the world (Keenan & Ward, 2003).

Thornton (2000; 2002) and Ward and Beech (2004) have described a framework of dynamic risk that includes:

- Sexual deviance.
- Distorted attitudes.
- Socio-affective functioning.
- Self-management.

Given the importance of family and peer groupings on adolescents, a fifth domain should also be included:

- Influential others.

Useful questions for each of these domains include:

- How much has this factor played a role in the young person's sexual aggression?
- If you took this factor out of the youth's aggression, would it have been less likely to occur? Would it have happened at all?
- To what extent does this factor have a role in the youth's general functioning?

The domains are considered in more detail. Much of what follows is adapted from Thornton (2000, 2004), Thornton & Prescott (2001), and Prescott (2006):

Sexual deviance. In this instance, deviance refers to the range and intensity of factors driving an adolescent's harmful sexual behavior. This can include elements of the youth's functioning that are markedly unusual when compared to non-abusive adolescents, that contribute to harmful behaviors, or that will bring them into conflict with themselves, others, society, and the law.

Professionals should consider this domain only with great caution. The sexual arousal patterns of adolescents are more fluid and dynamic than those of adults (Hunter & Becker, 1994; Hunter, 1999). Further, given that adolescence is a time when sex and sexuality are salient themes for all adolescents, adults can overestimate their role in the long term. What may appear sexually deviant may simply be a willingness to break rules, expressed through harmful sexual behavior. This is not intended to downplay the impact of sexual abuse on its victims, but to underscore the importance of differentiating the elements that contribute to sexual abuse. Finally, while true sexual pre-occupation is clearly important to understand, it can easily be overestimated in youth, for whom a level of pre-occupation can be considered normative.

Key questions to ask are:
- What is the direction of the young person's sexual interest?
- How narrowly is that interest defined?
- What is the intensity of that interest?

Professionals can consider three forms of sexual deviance:
- *Sexual preference for children* refers to the youth's having a stronger response to those significantly younger (by four or five years).
- *Sexualized violence* refers to either a preference for coerced sex or a strong sexual response to the victim's pain, suffering, or fear.
- *Sexual preoccupation* refers to the intensity of the youth's sexual interest. How much time do they spend thinking about sex? Do they think about sex to such an extent that it becomes

uncomfortable or has caused them concern? Do they engage in frequent indiscriminate and diverse sexual behaviors? Do they regularly masturbate several times a day? Do they regularly use or collect pornography over and above what would be considered normal for a teenager? How difficult is it to let go of a sexual idea once it has occurred? While none of these in themselves defines preoccupation, the guiding principle is that it is over and above what one would expect to find in an adolescent.

Distorted attitudes/contributory attitudes. This refers to the permission-giving self-statements that precede sexual aggression. It is important to note that this includes the attitudes *before* the incidents of sexual aggression, and not the defensive statements made afterwards ("I didn't think I'd get caught"). Caution should be taken in their assessment because, although they can be easy to treat, they can also be easy to hide. Examples include:

- *Sexual entitlement.* The belief that having a sexual desire entitles one to gratify it can be common in sexually abusive youth, as is the belief that their sex drive is stronger than others (e.g., "You don't understand: I'm a very sexual person"). Central to entitlement is the belief that one has a right to satisfy their sexual urges.

- *Child sexual abuse supportive beliefs.* This involves seeing much younger children as peers, and the belief that children can consent to sex. In some cases the youth may believe that his actions are of benefit to the child or that the child is interested in sex.

- *Rape minimization.* This includes the idea that others enjoy or want to be raped.

- *Rape justification.* This includes the belief that others deserve to be raped, especially when they behave badly. This belief is sometimes seemingly absent in normal functioning but activated when the young person is upset, angry, or anxious.

- *Seeing others as deceitful* can correspond with a world view that others are deceitful or manipulative, and that the youth has to fight back to gain the respect and safety they deserve. It can also correspond with a world view that the world is cold, hostile, or out of control.

Interpersonal/Socio-Affective functioning is essentially the relationship of the young person to the world around him, himself, and his future. It includes both relationships to others and perceptions of one's self within the context of these relationships:

- *Dysfunctional evaluation of self worth* includes an emotionally painful or negative view of one's identity and ongoing functioning. Conversely it can be an ongoing sense of pride based on anti-social characteristics. It can also include a narcissistic self-image that combines an explicit, conscious evaluation of one's self that is arrogant or grandiose but fragile, unstable, and vulnerable to injury. When threatened, a negative self-appraisal can be quickly activated.

- *Dysfunctional evaluation of self-efficacy* includes inaccurate perceptions that the youth has no control over his current or future behavior, and that other individuals and situations are responsible for his actions. The youth may engage in passive behaviors and view himself as helpless.

- *Lack of emotionally intimate relationships* includes youth who, for a variety of reasons, are neither able to establish healthy and stable peer relationships or dating relationships.

- *Emotional congruence with younger children* involves an adolescent feeling that it is easier to engage in relationships with much younger others.

- *Callousness/shallow emotions* includes a combination of callous and ruthless behaviors towards others in the absence of any strong emotions. While many youth do not appear to demonstrate guilt, remorse, or empathy in clinical interviews, a key feature of this is its duration across time and situation. Youths for whom this factor is prominent often fail to accept responsibility for their actions and demonstrate a lack of concern for the rights and welfare of others to an extent that is unusual even among other sexually abusive youth. This is the equivalent of the affective facet in Hare's (2003) four-facet model of psychopathy.

- *Grievance thinking* involves both an active belief that one is a victim of others and a persistent scanning of one's environment in search of potential threats. It can provide a sense of justification for harming others. It can often motivate behavior that leads to high-risk situations.

Self-management refers to the youth's ability to manage their behavior in a way that reflects long-term goals rather than short-term gratification.

- *Lifestyle impulsivity* includes behavior patterns that do not reflect healthy self-regulation. Impulsivity can range from failure to manage impulses (e.g., blurting out the answers in class) to an ongoing pervasive failure to consider the effects of one's actions on others and one's self. It also refers to reckless and irresponsible behavior as described in factor two of the *Psychopathy Checklist: Youth Version* (Forth, Kosson, & Hare, 2003).

- *Dysfunctional coping* refers to recurrent difficulties dealing with stress or other problems. It might include over-reliance on only a handful of coping skills that become ineffective over time. It can include over-reliance on sexual behavior as a coping mechanism. Dysfunctional coping can include the following:
  - Poor cognitive problem solving.
  - Poor problem anticipation.
  - Continued engagement in problem behavior despite obvious consequences.
  - Affective dysregulation, including irritability or other easily triggered negative affect.
  - Emotional rumination, where the youth copes with stress by persistently ruminating upon it in a negative way.
  - Avoidant coping, where the youth attempts to manage stress by avoiding it.

Poor executive functioning. In some cases, prefrontal cortex disturbances or deficits can contribute to poor self-management.

Influential others. Key questions are whether peers or family members actively support sexual aggression, or whether they might
tacitly support sexual abuse by ignoring risk situations or treatment recommendations.

Once these dynamic factors have been assessed through file
review and clinical interview, each domain can be discussed in the
body of the report, along with any information on how they interact. From this a list of treatment targets can be generated that may
help concerned adults provide services. An example of this is provided in the sample report in Appendix A.

What tools are available?

The field of assessing and treating sexually abusive youth has seen
many tools become available in the last two decades. There is no
shortage of measures, especially self-report forms, that are absent
of psychometric properties. Many of these scales appear to measure aspects such as sexual interests or anger, but in the absence of
formal study may simply reflect how the youth chose to answer
the questions that day. In some cases, youth may simply play
games with the forms by filling them out randomly or deliberate-
ly choosing the most egregious answer. Although they can be useful in treatment settings, professionals assessing youth are urged
to be cautious with self-report measures.

There remains no empirically validated method for accurate classification of risk, although three scales, the JSOAP – II, the J-SOR-
RAT – II, and the ERASOR show promise. Professionals are urged
to keep current with the research in this area, as many older tools
still in use have no empirical support. The following is an
overview of some tools, in varying stages of development, which
may be of use to professionals assessing sexually abusive youth.

Because young people are, on average, at greater risk for generally delinquent crimes, measures that look at the risks and needs of adolescent offenders in general can be helpful. Two such tools are the *Youth Level of Service/Case Management Inventory* and the *Jesness Behavior Checklist*.

Youth Level of Service/Case Management Inventory (YLS/CMI)

According to its authors, the YLS/CMI (Hoge & Andrews, 2003) "is designed to aid professionals in assessing adolescent male and female offenders. Probation officers, youth workers, psychologists, and social workers are among those who might make use of this instrument. YLS/CMI is a checklist that produces a detailed survey of the risk and need factors of the youth. It provides linkage between these factors and the development of a case plan" (p.1). The YLS/CMI is essentially a youth version adapted from the Level of Service Inventory – Revised (Andrews & Bonta, 1995). The YLS/CMI reflects a theory of risk and need described throughout its manual. Scores in eight categories contribute to estimates of risk based upon a sample of 314 young offenders aged twelve to seventeen (p. 6). The YLS/CMI is available to a wide range of professionals and can be helpful in case formulation.

Jesness Behavior Checklist (JBC)

The JBC is a measure consisting of self-appraisal and observer checklists. There are 80 items in each checklist, and it is expected that the youth and their observers can score it in a few minutes' time. It is "designed to provide a systematic way of recording data about social behavior. The checklist was originally developed for use with juvenile delinquents in institutions but has been modified to enable its use with persons of any age in a variety of settings" (p. 1). It can provide insight into a youth's functioning at home, in school, and in the community. It provides a window into the behavior of a young person, and can be useful in determining treatment targets. The JBC is available to a wide range of professionals. The JBC can be useful in gathering behavioral information where little is available.

YLS/CMI, the JBC, and the related *"Jesness Inventory – Revised"* are available from Multi-Health Systems at www.mhs.com.

Three key assessment methods specific to sexually abusive youth are The JSOAP-II, The Protective Factors Scale (PFS) and the ERASOR.

Juvenile Sex Offender Assessment Protocol-II (JSOAP-II):

The JSOAP-II (Prentky & Righthand, 2003) is regarded by many as an actuarial scale in that it contains fixed and explicit rules for scoring and weighting items. However, it has not yet been cross-validated and was developed on a small sample of ninety-six youth, of whom seventy-five were followed up, including three recidivists at one year. According to its authors, the JSOAP-II "is a checklist whose purpose is to aid in the systematic review of risk factors that have been identified in the professional literature as being associated with sexual *and criminal* offending (emphasis added, p. i)". Second, given that total scores on this instrument have yet to demonstrate significant predictive validity, one must use extreme caution in interpreting its results. The scales themselves may better address areas of need than the total score. Rather than viewing the JSOAP-II as a scale that predicts re-offense, professionals may do better to consider it as a method for addressing treatment needs and their severity.

JSOAP-II is currently available from the website of the Center for Sex Offender Management at www.csom.org.

Of the four scales, the second ("impulsive, antisocial behavior") constellation correlated the most highly with recidivism in the small research sample. Of note, the authors initially modeled this scale on the Child and Adolescent Taxon Scale (Quinsey, Harris,

Rice, & Cormier, 1998). Also known by its acronym, the CATS was developed as a substitute for Psychopathy Checklist – Revised, (PCL-R; Hare, 1991) scores in the Violence Risk Appraisal Guide, or (VRAG; Quinsey et al., 1998). In this case, the CATS proved to be effective, easy to score from file review and/or self-report, and for many applications can be more cost-effective than the PCL-R. More recently, the CATS was used to provide evidence of an underlying antisociality taxon among children (Skilling, Quinsey, & Craig, 2001).

The "sexual drive/preoccupation" scale correlated less with recidivism in the development sample. Its authors have since observed that in its original form it "performs suboptimally" (Righthand, Prentky, Knight, Carpenter, Hecker, & Nangle, 2005). Reasons for this are not known. It may be speculated that the nature of the youths' sexual crimes, fantasies, and drives result in many of the more dangerous youths not being released from institutions and therefore unavailable for follow-up. It may also be that the small sample sizes and brief follow-up periods in various studies have played a role. Hanson and Bussiere (1998) found that, on average, rapists recidivated more rapidly than child molesters. Hecker, Scoular, Righthand, & Nangle (2002) found in a ten-to twelve-year follow-up that total JSOAP scores were not correlated with sexual recidivism, but that scale one ("sexual drive") was very strongly predictive, albeit with a sample of only 6 recidivists (11%) in a sample of 54 male adolescents. However, Righthand, Knight, and Prentky (2002) found that higher scores on the sexual drive scale were associated with male victims and number of victims, while the antisocial behavior scale was associated with teenage and older victims. Clearly, the numbers reported are astronomically low. However, they do suggest beginning avenues for further inquiry in understanding these scales.

JSOAP-II can be an effective aid to those assessing risk among youth. Clinical items such as remorse, guilt and cognitive distortions are included but not weighted heavily when compared to historical items. Unfortunately, the specific role of these clinical items is not discussed fully. Many evaluators have met youth who freely admit their offenses out of pride and the arousal associated with recalling them. Other evaluators are familiar with the fact that strongly expressed remorse in a clinical interview does not mean that the same remorse will prevent future offenses (see the item description for remorse in Hare, 1991). Similarly, an internal motivation for change for all of us can change with time.

The JSOAP-II is relatively easy to score and contains many items associated with juvenile recidivism in the literature. It has become widely used in understanding sexually abusive youth in many quarters. Like the SVR-20 and HCR-20 it can contribute to a common expression of findings and methods of treatment planning among groups of clinicians and other service providers.

FIGURE 1: Items in the *Juvenile Sex Offender Assessment Protocol-II (JSOAP-II)*:

These items cannot properly be scored without the instructions that are available from the manual.

Factor 1: Sexual Drive/Preoccupation

- Prior legally charged sex offenses
- Number of sexual abuse victims
- Male child victim
- Duration of sex offense history
- Degree of planning in sex offenses
- Sexualized aggression
- Sexual drive and pre-occupation
- Sexual victimization history

Factor 2: Impulsive, Antisocial Behavior

- Caregiver instability
- Pervasive anger

- School behavior problems
- History of Conduct Disorder
- Juvenile antisocial behavior
- Ever charged/arrested before age 16
- Multiple types of offenses
- Physical assault history and/or exposure to family violence

Factor 3: Intervention

- Accepting responsibility for offenses
- Internal motivation for change
- Understands risk factors
- Remorse and guilt
- Cognitive distortions
- Quality of peer relationships

Factor 4: Community stability/Adjustment (past six months)

- Management of sexual urges and desire
- Management of anger
- Stability of current living situation
- Stability in school
- Evidence of support systems

The Protective Factors Scale (PFS):

This scale, and a chapter on its development, is available in Bremer (2006a and 2006b). It examines areas that serve to protect youth from further sexual misconduct. Although the instrument remains in development, it is a departure from "risk" assessment.

By emphasizing those factors that *mitigate* risk, the PFS lends itself to a broad range of treatment approaches and strength-based risk management strategies.

In a draft version, Bremer (2001) states:

> The Protective Factors Scale was initially designed as a way to evaluate the adequacy of initial placement orders for treatment (Bremer, 1998). The results of the pilot study indicate that the PFS can help determine at what level of placement a youth would successfully complete treatment. It is a placement tool that fits a unique niche. Community safety involves more than simply sexual recidivism. A means of where to place a youth on a continuum of care (Bengis, 1997) is quite useful. The continuum of care places a youth on a range of service from short-term psychoeducational community-based through intensive outpatient treatment, placement in the community, placement out of the community and correctional secure placement (p.1).

With the PFS, Bremer emphasizes that thinking exclusively in terms of "risk" is not sufficient to reduce that risk. Many users resonate with the focus on those factors that prevent youth from re-offense. Others find this in keeping with Andrews and Bonta's (2003) recommendation that the principles of need and responsivity be considered alongside risk.

FIGURE 2: items currently in *The Protective Factors Scale (PFS)*:

These items cannot properly be scored without the instructions that are available from the manual. These items are included only to encourage readers to consider protective factors in assessments of risk.

Factor 1: Sexuality

- Identified concern characteristics
- Personal boundaries
- Sexual preferences

Factor 2: Personal Development

- General behavior
- School attendance
- Social adjustment
- Emotional adjustment

Factor 3: Environmental Support

- Caregiver stability
- Family style
- Cooperation

The Protective Factors Scale is easy to use and emphasizes elements that can help prevent sexual recidivism by building on the strengths of the youth, their family, and community. In this way, it can contribute meaningfully to risk reduction strategies and methods. Initial results show that it can be effective in decisions regarding level of care. It contains items related both to increased risk and the healthy development of youth. Beyond its use as a scale, it can serve as a useful group of elements for clinicians to consider in developing treatment plans and interventions. It can help define treatment goals as areas to work towards (e.g., interpersonal fulfillment) rather than areas to avoid (e.g., relapse). It should not be used in isolation from other assessment methods.

Estimate of Risk of Adolescent Sex Offender Recidivism (ERASOR)

Its introduction clearly states that "The ERASOR is designed to assist evaluators to estimate the risk of a sexual reoffense ONLY for individuals aged 12-18 who have previously committed a sexual assault". Modeled on scales such as the PCL-R, HCR-20, SVR-20, where items are scored as present, absent, and partially/possibly present, the ERASOR is an example of an empirically grounded structured risk assessment method. Although the items in figure 3 may appear easy to score, many require a great deal of consideration and require adherence to the descriptions in the manual.

The ERASOR is constructed so that the total score is not the primary consideration. As its authors point out, the presence of only one risk factor may, under certain circumstances, be enough to warrant a determination of high risk. Although it is designed specifically to assess risk of sexual re-offense, a recent study (Bourgon, 2002) concluded that while the ERASOR assesses static factors related to sexual aggression, its dynamic factors are related to general delinquency. There has not been a large-scale study of the ERASOR's predictive validity.

Advantages of the ERASOR include the ability to consider a wide range of information in forming impressions and recommendations. It can be used for evaluation, treatment planning, and service delivery. Like other structured assessment methods, it enables the use of a common language among groups of clinicians. Many of the items have the potential to be used for evaluating treatment outcomes.

Perhaps the greatest advantage of the ERASOR is its manual and the item descriptions themselves, which provide an extensive overview of the literature as well as the difficulties inherent in adolescent sexual abuser risk assessment.

This tool is available from its principle author, James Worling, The Safe-T Program, Thistletown Regional Centre, 51 Panorama Court, Toronto, Ontario, Canada, M9V 4L8. Email: jworling@ican.net.

FIGURE 3: Items from *Estimate of Risk of Adolescent Sex Offender Recidivism (ERASOR)*

The item descriptions are of primary importance. The items below are included only to give the reader a rough idea of areas to be assessed in the ERASOR.

- Deviant sexual interest (younger children, violence, or both)

- "Obsessive" sexual interests/preoccupation with sexual thoughts
- Attitudes supportive of sexual offending
- Unwillingness to alter deviant sexual interests/attitudes
- Ever assaulted 2 or more victims
- Ever assaulted same victim 2 or more times
- Prior adult sanctions for sexual assault(s)
- Threats of, or use of, violence/weapons during sexual offense
- Ever sexually assaulted a child
- Ever sexually assaulted a stranger
- Indiscriminate choice of victims
- Ever sexually assaulted a male victim (male offenders only)
- Diverse sexual-assault behaviors
- Antisocial interpersonal orientation
- Lack of intimate peer relationships/social isolation
- Negative peer associations and influences
- Interpersonal aggression
- Recent escalation in anger or negative affect
- Poor self-regulation of affect and behavior (Impulsivity)
- High-stress family environment
- Problematic parent-offender relationships/parental rejection
- Parent(s) not supporting sexual-offense-specific assessment/treatment
- Environment supporting opportunity to offend
- No development or practice of realistic prevention plans/strategies
- Incomplete offense-specific treatment

The items in the ERASOR reflect several possible pathways to re-offense. In keeping with current research, these can include pathways reflective of an emerging sexual disorder, antisociality, or chronic detachment (Roberts, Doren, & Thornton, 2002). It includes both static and dynamic factors, including those that are relatively stable over time (e.g., incomplete offense-specific treatment) and those that can change acutely and rapidly (e.g., recent escalation in anger or negative affect). The manual provides a comprehensive yet succinct set of descriptions of the individual items.

The Structured Assessment of Violence Risk in Youth (SAVRY)

The SAVRY (Borum, Bartel, & Forth, 2002) is an empirically grounded method for assessing violence risk (including sexual violence) in adolescents. Its structure is similar to the ERASOR, in that it contains items established in the literature as being associated with violence, each of which are scored as present, absent, or partially/possibly present. Preliminary psychometric data are provided. Like the ERASOR, it is intended as a guide for professionals, and not to provide a total score with cutoffs for risk classification. It contains:

- Ten *historical* items (related to age of onset, history of violence, failure to comply with supervision, etc.)
- Six *contextual* items (such as the presence or absence of parental support, quality of peer relationships, ability to cope, etc.)
- Eight *individual* items (presence of ADHD, low remorse or empathy, low commitment to school, etc.)
- Six *protective* items (e.g., strong social supports, resilient personality, positive attitude towards intervention, etc.)

The SAVRY is available from www.specializedtraining.com and from http://fmhi.usf.edu.

The Hare Psychopathy Checklist: Youth Version (PCL: YV)

A full description of psychopathy and its measurement is beyond the scope of this primer. Although originally intended as a measure of the construct of psychopathy, scores on the Hare Psychopathy Checklist – Revised (Hare, 1991) have been found to be predictive of violence, criminality, and when combined with sexual deviance, sexual recidivism in adult populations. There was great anticipation of the release of the PCL: YV (Forth, Kosson, & Hare, 2003).

Among adults, psychopathy can be a powerful predictor of harmful behavior. However, extending this construct to youth can be problematic. Many have taken note that even normal adolescents can display psychopathic traits. Ultimately, youth can change in ways that adults can't predict. The seemingly psychopathic 16-year-old can look remarkably better even a year later. Ethical issues with the construct and even use of the word "psychopath" can convince a professional to avoid consideration of it altogether. Were it not for the importance of the construct, this might even be advisable. Ultimately, those attempting to understand adolescent sexual aggression are obligated to have some knowledge of the construct. *Robert Hare's Page for the Study of Psychopaths, "Sociopaths", Violent Offenders, Serial Killers* ... (www.hare.org) maintains a list of upcoming workshops, as well as a bibliography related to psychopathy.

The PCL: YV is a psychological test that requires special qualifications to administer. Those unable to purchase and administer it should still develop knowledge of the construct and make referrals for assessment as needed. It is published by Multi-Health systems, and available at www.mhs.com or www.parinc.com.

Viewing Time

The use of phallometry (i.e. the penile plethysmograph – a means of examining sexual arousal patterns by measuring blood flow through the penis in response to stimuli) with adolescents has seen a decline in recent years. This decline may be due to concerns about its intrusiveness and the ethics of exposing youth to sexually oriented material. The dynamic nature of sexual arousal across adolescence has also led many professionals to question its benefits in relationship to its costs. While there is no doubt a time and place for phallometry with older adolescents, there are numerous situations where its use is inappropriate (Letourneau & Prescott, 2005).

Viewing time measures examine, among other things, how long a subject looks at an image on a screen. The underlying theory is that people look at things they are attracted to longer than those they are not. The most widely distributed, and first commercially available viewing time measure is the Abel Assessment of Sexual Interest (sometimes referred to as the Abel Screen). Notice the term "interest" as viewing time purports to measure interest and not physical arousal.

While neither instrument can measure an individual's willingness to engage in harmful sexual behavior, nor help determine guilt or innocence, viewing time such as the Abel Screen can provide useful information for assessment and treatment purposes within the parameters in which they have been established. Critics of viewing time assert that it is built on too many inferences to be used in forensic settings, and note that the language involved (e.g., "probability values") can be misleading. Critics note that the data involved in its construction have not been shared to any great extent with other researchers. Proponents note that when used appropriately, viewing time can be helpful and significantly less intrusive than phallometry. They also note that it can be used in numerous applications where the plethysmograph cannot, such as screening those working with youth in high-sensitivity situations.

For more information, readers can visit www.abelscreen.com.

The Juvenile Sex Offense Recidivism Risk Assessment Tool – II (JSORRAT – II)

The JSORRAT-II (Epperson, Ralston, Fowers, DeWitt, & Gore, 2006) is an actuarial tool developed on a sample of 636 youth adjudicated for a sexual offense in Utah between 1990 and 1992. Despite the exhaustive nature of the sample, this instrument has not yet been validated on an independent sample. Preliminary findings suggest it is more effective in predicting recidivism in adolescence than adulthood. It consists of twelve easily-scored historical items. These are provided below although, like the other scales, the items cannot be used without referring to the manual for instructions on scoring and weighting them:

- Number of adjudications for sex offenses (including current adjudication).
- Number of different victims in charged sex offenses.
- Length of sexual offending history based on charged sex offenses.
- Under any form of supervision when they committed any sex offense for which they were eventually charged?
- Was any charged felony-level sex offense committed in a public place?
- Use of deception or grooming in any charged sex offense?
- Prior sex offender treatment status.
- Number of officially documented incidents of hands-on sexual abuse in which the offender was the victim.
- Number of officially documented incidents of physical abuse where the offender was the victim.
- Any placement in special education?
- Number of education time periods with discipline problems.
- Number of adjudications for non-sexual offenses.

The JSORRAT-II is promising. Its items derive from careful data analysis and reflect findings from elsewhere in the research on youth who have sexually abused. Validation on an independent sample could result in an effective screening measure that can inform treatment planning.

Trauma Assessment

Finally, it can be useful to address trauma symptoms as a means of assessing treatment need, readiness, and responsivity.

Trauma Symptom Checklist for Children (TSCC)

There is increasing evidence that trauma plays a role in the etiology of sexual abuse. Further, treatment providers often find themselves balancing the seemingly competing needs of addressing trauma while reducing the likelihood of future harmful behaviors. The TSCC (Briere, 1996) is useful in diverse situations, including in the absence of information on trauma history, or where there are concerns about a young person's ability to engage in the treatment process.

The TSCC is a self-report checklist designed for use with young people ages eight through sixteen years. It can be used by individuals who do not have formal training in clinical psychology. The TSCC is available from www.parinc.com.

Other Assessments

In many situations, assessing the youth exclusively will miss other useful avenues. Family assessments can yield important information for getting youth and family back on track (Schladale, 2006; Thomas & Viar, 2006). Current understanding into the neurological impact of trauma requires that professionals consider a neuropsychological assessment and assessment of learning disabilities in order to properly match available services to the needs of the youth. The importance of understanding comorbid conditions cannot be understated.

Report Writing

The form and content of an assessment report will depend on the referral question, the youth, and his situation. A sample template and report are provided in Appendix A. Assessment reports generally contain an overview of the referral question, any measures used, a history of the concerns to be addressed, and a description of the context within which they have occurred. The author then discusses their impressions and conclusions, and makes recommendations. A common mistake is to include new information in the latter sections. Professionals should introduce material early in the report so that the reader is better able to follow the logic of the author.

Because youth who have sexually abused are more likely to be arrested for non-sexual crimes, professionals will wish to consider their risk for violence, general criminality, and in some cases, suicide. A helpful structure for presenting material in a report can be to divide each of these areas into three aspects: *historical* (or static) variables that are fixed in the young person's history (e.g. early onset and persistence); *dynamic* (or potentially changeable) factors, which can serve as risk markers and treatment targets; and *protective factors*, which serve to mitigate risk and which can serve as a starting point from which service providers can work.

By the time many assessors are producing their reports, they have long forgotten the rules of writing they learned in high school. Some may never have learned them at all. In order to have influence in whatever setting a report appears, it is strongly recommended that professionals review some basic rules of writing:

- Avoid the passive voice.
- The strength of language is in nouns and verbs, *not* adjectives.
- The first words in a sentence are the most important.
- Avoid words ending in "ly".

- Always review a printed copy of your report.
- Review your report from the vantage point of diverse victims and attorneys.
- Have a supervisor or colleague review your report in accordance with confidentiality requirements.
- Word-processing spell checkers are helpful, but beware of incorrect replacement "suggestions".

Specifically, reports on sexually abusive youth:

- Consider the body of a report a vehicle for leading the reader to obvious conclusions.
- May contain a summary of findings on the first page of the report.
- Avoid jargon (e.g., "issue", "dynamic", "cycle") and overuse of initials ("CSA", "SAY").
- Contain an explicit recounting of the referral question.
- Are specific in content (e.g., "Mr. X has a number of victims" is less helpful than a specific number or accounting of victims).
- Contain a narrative that not only describes the youth's history, but also describes elements of their life that readers need to know.
- Present as many facts, and as little opinion, as possible. A good report leads its audience to incontrovertible conclusions.
- Use neither vague language (e.g., "fondled", when "squeezed and twisted" would be more accurate) nor stilted ("his treatment progress has been abysmal" versus "he has not made gains in treatment, as evidenced by…").
- Avoid pejorative terms (e.g., "predator", "psychopath") whose meanings are not specific.
- Prefer simple language to vague or legalistic ("he forced her to engage in vaginal intercourse" is preferable to "he raped her").

- Are specific with editorial (e.g., "issue-specific treatment can help Biff reduce his risk for harmful sexual behaviors" is preferable to "he is dangerous without treatment").
- Protect victim confidentiality.
- Stay within one's area of expertise.

Here are some examples. The first is adapted from a newspaper account, but illustrates common errors:

> "In May 2003, it was announced that Mr. K, 21, had been criminally charged by the County District Attorney with a violation of Wis. Stat. 948.02(2) and 939.50(3)(c) which establishes criminal punishment for sexual contact with a child under the age of sixteen."

Note the passive voice and legal language, which obscures the crime. The sentence highlights the fact that the law "establishes criminal punishment" rather than the fact that Mr. K may well have committed a crime. This might have been said more simply:

> "The County District Attorney has alleged that Mr. K, aged 21, had sex with a person under the age of 16."

In sentence structure, it may be best to simply start at the beginning:

> "When he was done hitting her, he…" can be replaced by "He then…" where it is already obvious that "he hit her."

A useful axiom might be to use key language at the start if you can, and at the end if you cannot.

Finally, it is important to note that little words have meaning, too:

> "He threatened her life and had intercourse with her."
>
> implies a relationship, while "He threatened her life and forced her to engage in intercourse" does not.

Finally, the work of Strunck and White (2000) may be useful:

> Do not overstate:
> When you overstate, readers will be instantly on guard, and everything that has preceded your overstatement and everything that follows will be suspect in their

minds because they have lost confidence in your judge-
ment or your poise (p. 73).

Do not overwrite:
Rich, ornate prose is hard to digest, generally unwhole-
some, and sometimes nauseating...you must guard
against wordiness. The click and flow of a word proces-
sor can be seductive. It is always a good idea to reread
your writing later and ruthlessly delete the excess (p. 72).

Place yourself in the background:
To achieve style, begin by affecting none - that is, place
yourself in the background. A careful and honest writer
does not need to worry about style. Fortunately, the act
of composition, or creation, disciplines the mind; writing
is one way to go about thinking, and the practice and
habit of writing not only drain the mind but supply it,
too (p. 70).

Be clear:
When you become hopelessly mired in a sentence, it is
best to start fresh; do not try to fight your way through
the terrible odds of syntax. Usually what is wrong is that
the construction has become too involved at some point;
the sentence needs to be broken apart and replaced by
two or more shorter sentences (p. 79).

Do not inject opinion:
Unless there is a good reason for its being there, do not
inject opinion into a piece of writing. We all have opinions about almost everything, and the temptation to toss
them in is great... Opinions scattered indiscriminately
about, leave the mark of egotism on a work (pp. 79-80).

Finally, it is important to watch for all forms of minimization:

- "He reports that in the past he would..." versus "He has..."

- "He has deviant arousal patterns." versus "He is aroused by
  children."

- "His index offense involved the sexual assault of a six-year-
  old girl. Records indicate that she was both vaginally and
  anally penetrated" versus "He forced vaginal and anal inter-

course on his most recent victim, a six-year-old girl."

- "Force and violence were involved in the offense" versus "He used force and violence during the offense" (and specifying the force and violence will make the sentence even stronger, although sometimes this information is not properly clarified in the original reports).

- "CSA" versus "child sexual abuse"

Reports should make clear recommendations for the next steps adults can take. Recommending "sex offender treatment" is vague; recommending specific treatment targets (e.g., interpersonal skills, attitudes that support sexual abuse, self-management skills) can contribute meaningfully to future efforts. Likewise, simply recommending a "psychiatric evaluation" is not helpful, while posing specific questions for such a referral can be crucial to a young person's success.

Conclusion

In its broadest sense, assessment is a fundamental aspect of human existence and survival. It can range from social judgment to carefully constructed processes relying on multiple sources of information, objective measures, and a base of evidence. Successful assessment of youth who have sexually abused begins with understanding the available tools, possible assessment processes, normative adolescent development, and the current research into all aspects of assessment. These elements, as well as the use of the tools described earlier, can serve as lenses to place information into a proper, and helpful, perspective. Professionals can promote accuracy by attending to the basics, such as clarifying the referral question, sharpening their interviewing skills, and paying close attention to their communication methods.

Understanding and assessing any human being, especially young people, can fascinate and reward those who work at it. Being trusted to listen to a young person's story is an honor in itself. Discovering the limitations of our ability to understand accurately, while frustrating, is a necessary aspect of this endeavor. Although our field has much to learn to optimize our assessments of young people, professionals are urged to keep abreast of developments in the field, and take the opportunity to consult with each other on how best to improve their abilities. The future of our youth deserves no less.

References

Alexander, M. (1999). Sexual offender treatment efficacy revisited. *Sexual Abuse: A Journal of Research and Treatment, 11,* 101-116.

Andrews, D.A. & Bonta, J.L. (1995). *Manual for the Level of Service Inventory- Revised.* Toronto: Multi-Health Systems, Inc.

Andrews, D.A. & Bonta, J.L. (2003). *The psychology of criminal conduct, Third edition.* Cincinnati: Anderson Publishing.

Bengis, S. (1997). Comprehensive service delivery in a continuum of care. In G. Ryan & S. Lane (Eds.), *Juvenile sexual offending: Causes, consequences, and correction* (pp. 211-218). San Francisco: Jossey-Bass.

Borum, R., Bartel, P., & Forth, A.E. (2002). *Manual for the structured assessment of violence risk in youth.* Tampa, Florida: University of South Florida. Available at http://fmhi.usf.edu/.

Bourgon, G. (2002). *The Estimate of Risk of Adolescent Sex Offender Recidivism (ERASOR): Evaluating its psychometric properties.* Paper presented at the Annual Meeting of the Association for the Treatment of Sexual Abusers, Montreal, Quebec, Canada.

Bremer, (1998). Challenges in the assessment and treatment of sexually abusive adolescents, *Irish Journal of Psychology,* 19 (1) 82-92.

Bremer, J.F. (2001). *The Protective Factors Scales: assessing youth with sexual concerns.* Plenary addresses at the 16th annual conference of the National Adolescent Perpetration Network, Kansas City, Mo. May 7, 2001.

Bremer, J.F. (2006a). Building resilience: An ally in assessment and treatment. In D.S. Prescott (Ed.), *Risk assessment of youth who have sexually abused: Theory, controversy, and emerging strategies* (pp. 87-99). Oklahoma City, OK: Wood'N'Barnes.

Bremer, J.F. (2006b). The Protective Factors Scale. In D.S. Prescott (Ed.), *Risk assessment of youth who have sexually abused: Theory, controversy, and emerging strategies* (pp. 195-221). Oklahoma City, OK: Wood'N'Barnes.

Briere, J. (1996). *The Trauma Symptom Checklist for Children.* Lutz, FL: Psychological Assessment Resources.

Caldwell, M.F. (2002). What we do not know about juvenile sex offense risk assessment. *Child Maltreatment, 7,* 291-302.

Doren, D.M. (2002). *Evaluating Sex Offenders: A Manual for Civil Commitments and Beyond.* Thousand Oaks, Ca.: Sage.

Elliott, D.S. (1994). *The developmental course of sexual and non-sexual violence: Results from a national longitudinal study.* Paper presented at the meeting of the Association for the Treatment of Sexual Abusers' 13th Annual Research and Treatment Conference, San Francisco.

Epperson, D.L., Ralston, C.A., Fowers, D., DeWitt, J., & Gore, K.S. (2006, in press). Actuarial risk assessment with juveniles who offend sexually: Development of the Juvenile Sexual Offense Recidivism Risk Assessment Tool-II (JSOR-RAT-II). In D.S. Prescott (Ed.), *Risk assessment of youth who have sexually abused: Theory, controversy, and emerging strategies.* Oklahoma City, OK: Wood'N'Barnes.

Fernandez, Y. (2002). *In their shoes: Examining empathy and its place in the treatment of offenders.* Oklahoma City: Wood'N'Barnes.

Forth, A.E., Kosson, D.S., & Hare, R.D. (2003). *Psychopathy Checklist: Youth Version.* Toronto, Ontario, Canada: Multi-Health Systems.

Forth, A.E. & Mailloux, D.L. (2000) Psychopathy in youth: What do we know?, in Gacono, C.B. (Ed.) *The clinical and forensic assessment of psychopathy.* Mahwah, NJ: Lawrence Erlbaum Associates.

Gilgun, J.F. (2006). Children and adolescents with problematic sexual behaviors: lessons from research on resilience. In R.E. Longo & D.S. Prescott (Eds.), *Current perspectives: Working with sexually aggressive youth and youth with sexual behavior problems (pp.383-394)*. Holyoke, MA: NEARI Press.

Gray, A.S., & Wallace, R. (1992). *Adolescent sex offender packet*. Brandon, VT: Safer Society Press.

Hanson, R.K. (1997). The development of a brief actuarial risk scale for sexual offense recidivism. Department of the Solicitor General of Canada, Ottawa, Ontario.

Hanson, R.K. (2000). *Risk assessment*. Beaverton, Oregon: Association for the Treatment of Sexual Abusers.

Hanson, R.K., & Bussiere, M.T. (1998). Predicting relapse: a meta-analysis of sexual offender recidivism studies, *Journal of Consulting and Clinical Psychology, 66* (2), 348-362. Also available at http://www.psepc-sppcc.gc.ca/.

Hanson, R.K., & Harris, A.J.R. (2001). A structured approach to evaluating change among sexual offenders. *Sexual Abuse: A Journal of Research and Treatment, 13*(2), 105-122.

Hanson, R.K., & Morton-Bourgon, K.E. (2004). Predictors of sexual recidivism: An updated meta-analysis. Available at: http://www.psepc.gc.ca/publications/corrections/pdf/200402_e.pdf .

Hanson, R.K., & Thornton, D. (2000). Improving actuarial risk assessments for sex offenders. *Law and Human Behavior, 24*, 119-136.

Hare, R.D. (1991). *The Hare Psychopathy Checklist- Revised*. Toronto: Multi-Health Systems, Inc.

Hare, R.D. (2003). *The Hare Psychopathy Checklist- Revised II*. Toronto: Multi-Health Systems, Inc.

Hart, S.D., Cox, D., & Hare, R.D. (1995). *The Hare Psychopathy*

Checklist: Screening Version (PCL:SV). Toronto, Ontario: Multi-Health Systems.

Hecker, J. Scoular, J. Righthand, S., & Nangle, D. (2002, October). *Predictive validity of the J-SOAP over 10-plus years: Implications for risk assessment.* Paper presented at the Annual Meeting of the Association for the Treatment of Sexual Abusers, Montreal, Quebec, Canada.

Henggeler, S.W., Schoenwald, S.K., Borduin, C.M., Rowland, M.D., & Cunningham, P.B. (1998)

Hindman, J. (2005). *The best of times, the worst of time: Sex offender therapists and their costumes.* The ATSA Forum. Newsletter of the Association for the Treatment of Sexual Abusers.

Hoge, R.D., & Andrews, D.A. (2003). *Youth Level of Service/Case Management Inventory.* Toronto, Ontario, Canada: Multi-Health Systems.

Hunter, J. (1999). *Understanding juvenile sexual offending behavior: Emerging research, treatment approaches, and management practices.* Center for Sex Offender Management. Available at www.csom.org.

Hunter, J. (2006). Understanding diversity in juvenile sexual offenders: Implications for assessment, treatment, and legal management. In R.E. Longo & D.S. Prescott (Eds.), *Current perspectives: Working with sexually aggressive youth and youth with sexual behavior problems (pp. 63-78).* Holyoke, MA: NEARI Press.

Hunter, J.A. & Becker, J.V. (1994). The role of deviant sexual arousal in juvenile sexual offending: Etiology, evaluation, and treatment, *Criminal Justice and Behavior* 21, 132-149.

Hunter, J.A., & Figueredo, A.J. (1999). Factors associated with treatment compliance in a population of juvenile sexual offenders. *Sexual Abuse: A Journal of Research and Treatment, 11*, 49-68.

Jenkins, A. (2006). Discovering integrity: Working with shame without shaming young people who have sexually abused. In R.E. Longo & D.S. Prescott (Eds.), *Current perspectives: Working with sexually aggressive youth and youth with sexual behavior problems (pp. 419-443)*. Holyoke, MA: NEARI Press.

Jesness, C. (2004). *Jesness Behavior Checklist*. Toronto: Multi-Health Systems.

Keenan, T. & Ward, T. (2003). Developmental antecedents in sexual offending. In T. Ward, D.R. Laws, & S.M. Hudson (Eds.), *Sexual deviance: Issues and controversies* (pp. 119-134). Thousand Oaks, CA: Sage

Kenny, D.T., Keough, T., & Seidler, K. (2001). Predictors of recidivism in Australian juvenile sex offenders: Implications for treatment, *Sexual Abuse: A Journal of Research and Treatment, 13,* 131-148.

Knight, R.A. & Prentky, R. (1993). Exploring characteristics for classifying juvenile sex offenders. In H.E. Barbaree, W.L. Marshall, & S.M. Hudson (Eds.), *The juvenile sex offender* (pp. 45-83). New York: Guilford.

Lambie, I. & Robson, M. (2006). Words from the heart: The process of change with sexually abusive youth. In R.E. Longo & D.S. Prescott (Eds.), *Current perspectives: Working with sexually aggressive youth and youth with sexual behavior problems (pp. 625-638)*. Holyoke, MA: NEARI Press.

Langstrom, N., & Grann, M. (2000). Risk for criminal recidivism among young sex offenders, *Journal of Interpersonal Violence, 15,* 855-871.

Letourneau, E.J., & Prescott, D.S. (2005). Ethical issues in sex offender assessments. In S.W. Cooper, A.P. Giardano, V.I. Vieth, & N.D. Kellogg (Eds.), *Medical and legal aspects of child sexual exploitation: A comprehensive review of child pornography, child prostitution, and internet crimes against children*. St. Louis, MO: G.W. Medical Publishing.

Marczyk, G.R., Heilbrun, K., Lander, T., & DeMatteo, D. (2003). Predicting juvenile recidivism with the PCL:YV, MAYSI, and YLS/CMI, *International Journal of Forensic Mental Health, 2*, 7-18. Available at http://www.iafmhs.org/files/Marczyk.pdf.

Marshall, W.L., Fernandez, Y.M., Serran, G., Mulloy, R., Thornton, D., Mann, R.E. , & Anderson, D. (2003). Process variables in the treatment of sexual offenders: A review of the relevant literature. *Aggression and Violent Behavior, 8,* 205-234.

Miller, W.R., & Rollnick, S. (2002). *Motivational interviewing: Preparing people for change.* New York: Guilford.

Monahan, J. (1981/1995). *The clinical prediction of violent behavior.* Northvale, New Jersey: Jason Aronson Inc.

Monahan, J. Steadman, H.J. Silver, E., Applebaum, P.S., Robbins, P.C., Mulvey, E.P., Roth, L.H., Grisso, T., & Banks, S. (2001). *Rethinking risk assessment: The Macarthur study of violence and mental disorder.* New York: Oxford University Press.

Nisbet, I.A., Wilson, P.H., & Smallbone, S.W. (2004). A prospective longitudinal study of sexual recidivism among adolescent sex offenders. *Sexual Abuse: A Journal of Research and Treatment, 16*, 223-234.

Prentky, R. & Righthand, S. (2003). *Juvenile Sex Offender Assessment Protocol-II (JSOAP-II).* Available from Center for Sex Offender Management at www.csom.org.

Prescott, D.S. (2004). Emerging strategies for assessing risk : Theory, controversy, and practice. In R. Geffner, K.C. Franey, T.G. Arnold, & R. Falconer (Eds.), *Identifying and treating youth who sexually offend: Current approaches, techniques, and research* (pp. 83-106). Binghamton, NY: Haworth Press.

Prescott, D.S. (2005). The current state of adolescent risk assessment. In B. Schwartz (Ed). *The Sex Offender, Volume V* (pp. 17-1 – 17-15). New York: Civic Research Institute.

Prescott, D.S. (2006). *Risk assessment of youth who have sexually abused: Theory, controversy, and emerging strategies.* Oklahoma City, OK: Wood'N'Barnes.

Quinsey, V.L., Harris, G.T., Rice, M.E., & Cormier, C.A. (1998). *Violent Offenders: Managing and Appraising Risk.* Washington D.C.: American Psychological Association.

Quinsey, V.L. (2000) "The Violence Risk Appraisal Guide", Presentation at Sinclair Seminars' Sex Offender Re-Offense Risk Prediction Symposium, Madison, Wisconsin, March 2000. Available at www.sinclairseminars.com.

Quinsey, V.L., Skilling, T.A., Lalumiere, M.L., & Craig, W.M. (2004). *Juvenile delinquency: Understanding the origins of individual differences.* Washington, D.C.: American Psychological Association.

Righthand, S., Knight, R., & Prentky, R. (2002, October). *A path analytic investigation of proximal antecedents of J-SOAP risk domains.* Paper presented at the Annual Meeting of the Association for the Treatment of Sexual Abusers, Montreal, Quebec, Canada.

Righthand, S., Prentky, R., Knight, R., Carpenter, E., Hecker, J.E., & Nangle, D. (2005). Factor structure and validation of the Juvenile Sex Offender Protocol (JSOAP). *Sexual Abuse: A Journal of Research and Treatment, 17,* 13-30.

Roberts, C.F., Doren, D.M., & Thornton, D. (2002). Dimensions associated with sex offender recidivism risk. *Criminal Justice and Behavior, 29,* 569-589.

Ryan, G. (2005). Prevention in the next generation. *Journal of Interpersonal Violence, 20,* 132-141.

Schladale, J. (2006). Family matters: The importance of engaging families in treatment with sexually aggressive youth. In R.E. Longo & D.S. Prescott (Eds.), *Current perspectives: Working with sexually aggressive youth and youth with sexual behavior problems.* Holyoke, MA: NEARI Press.

Serin, R.C. & Brown, S.L. (2000). The clinical use of the Hare Psychopathy Checklist – Revised in contemporary risk assessment. In Gacono, C.G. (Ed.), *The Clinical and Forensic Assessment of Psychopathy* (pp. 251-268). Mahwah, NJ: Lawrence Erlbaum Associates.

Siegel, D.J. (1999). *The developing mind: Toward a neurobiology of interpersonal experience.* New York: Guilford Press.

Skilling, T.A., Quinsey, V.L., & Craig, W.M. (2001). Evidence of a taxon underlying serious antisocial behavior in boys, *Criminal Justice and Behavior, 28,* 450-470.

Strunk, W. & White, E.B. (2000). *The elements of style, Fourth edition.* Boston: Allyn and Bacon.

Tangney, J.P., & Dearing, R.L. (2002). *Shame and guilt.* New York: Guilford Press.

Thomas, J. & Viar, W. (2006). From family research to practice. In R.E. Longo & D.S. Prescott (Eds.), *Current perspectives: Working with sexually aggressive youth and youth with sexual behavior problems.* Holyoke, MA: NEARI Press.

Thornton, D. (2000). *Structured risk assessment,* Presentation at Sinclair Seminars' Sex Offender Re-Offense Risk Prediction Symposium, Madison, Wisconsin, March 2000. Available at www.sinclairseminars.com.

Thornton, D. (2002). Constructing and testing a framework for dynamic risk assessment. *Sexual Abuse: A Journal of Research and Treatment, 14,* 139-154.

Thornton, D. (2004, April). *Psychological factors underlying offending.* Workshop at Sand Ridge Secure Treatment Center, Mauston, Wisconsin, April 27, 2004.

Thornton, D., & Prescott, D.S. (2001). *Structured risk assessment: Youth version.* Unpublished manuscript.

Ward, T., & Beech, A.R. (2004). The etiology of risk: A preliminary model. *Sexual Abuse: A Journal of Research and Treatment, 16,* 271-284.

Ward, T., Day, A., Howells, K., & Birgden, A. (2004). The multifactor offender readiness model. *Aggression and Violent Behavior, 9,* 645-673.

Webster (2001). *Webster's New World Dictionary.* Springfield, MA: Webster's New World.

Webster, C.D., Ben-Aron, M.H., & Hucker, S.J. (1985). *Dangerousness: Probability and prediction, psychiatry and public policy.* Cambridge: Cambridge University Press.

Weinrott, M.R. (1996). *Juvenile sexual aggression: A critical review.* Boulder, CO: Center for the Study and Prevention of Violence.

Williams, M. (1975). Aspects of the psychology of imprisonment. In S. McConville, (Ed), *The use of imprisonment: Essays in the changing state of English penal policy* (pp. 32-42). London: Routledge & Kegan Paul Ltd.

Worling, J.R., & Curwen, T., (2000). *Estimate of Risk of Adolescent Sexual Offense Recidivism (ERASOR). Version 2.0.* Toronto, Canada: Safe-T Program, Thistletown Regional Centre for Children and Adolescents, Ontario Ministry of Community and Social Services.

Worling, J.R. (2004). The Estimate of Risk of Adolescent Sexual Offense Recidivism (ERASOR): Preliminary psychometric data. *Sexual Abuse: A Journal of Research and Treatment, 16,* 235-254.

Zamble, E., & Quinsey, V.L. (1997). *The criminal recidivism process.* New York: Cambridge University Press.

Zolondek, S.C., Abel, G.G., Northey, W.F., & Jordan, A.D. (2001). The self-reported behaviors of juvenile sex offenders. *Journal of Interpersonal Violence, 16,* 73-85.

APPENDIX A

The following report will hopefully serve as both a potential template and example of the use of language:

NEW SEAPORT YOUTH ACADEMY
NEW SEAPORT, CALISOTA

[A proper letterhead can make a report appear more authoritative, but are often neglected. Likewise, page numbers and a header can be useful, e.g., Axehandle Assessment, 5-14-93.]

SEXUAL AGGRESSION ASSESSMENT

NAME:	Biff Axehandle
DATE OF BIRTH:	November 1, 1976
DATE OF ADMISSION:	June 10, 1992
PRIMARY CLINICIAN:	Raven Desktop, LCSW
DATE OF REPORT:	May 14, 1993

BACKGROUND INFORMATION

Biff is a sixteen-year-old Asian-American male from New Seaport, Calisota. He was referred to New Seaport Youth Academy by Dimona County Public Schools Office. He is currently in his parents' custody. He is also currently on probation following a December 1992 conviction for simple assault, described below. More recently, he attempted to sexually assault a male peer and aggressively propositioned an adult male staff member. The concerned adults in Biff's life have requested an assessment of Biff's sexually abusive behavior for purposes of treatment planning and placement decisions. This report is intended for these contexts only, and should be used for these purposes only for the next six months to a year. Possible limitations of this report are discussed below. Because Biff's history of sexually abusive behavior contains elements of coercion, this report also discusses Biff's difficulties with interpersonal aggression.

Concerns upon Biff's admission to New Seaport Youth Academy (an intensively supervised residential facility) included termination from his previous educational placement following revelations that he had engaged in a number of acts of inappropriate sexual behavior with other younger, more vulnerable students. Biff has since acknowledged that these acts were coercive in nature. Other concerns included a history of impulsive and aggressive behaviors, reports that he had allegedly sexually abused a five-year-old neighborhood boy (although there was apparently no follow-up), Biff's special education status, difficulties managing anger, and poor social skills. Biff has been diagnosed with Bipolar Disorder, Attention Deficit Hyperactivity Disorder, and Learning Disorders.

RECORDS REVIEWED

This writer interviewed Biff and his parents on three occasions, (insert dates here). New Seaport Youth Academy documents including [insert list of documents here] were reviewed in the preparation of this report.

Pre-placement materials furnished upon admission were also reviewed, including:

[Insert list of pre-placement documentation here.]

MOST RECENT DIAGNOSIS/TESTING

A Psychiatric Evaluation Report by X, M.D. dated ___ provides the following diagnosis:

Axis I —

Axis II —

Axis III—

Axis IV —

Axis V —

Biff's medications are monitored and evaluated by X, M.D. His most recent medication review was February 5, 1993. He is currently prescribed:

[List medications here.]

Per a Psychological Evaluation dated ___, by Dr. Y, Biff's score's on the ___ were:

Verbal IQ -

Performance IQ -

Full-scale IQ -

The examiner noted that Biff displayed "low self-esteem... he experiences the world as threatening and is prone to lash out aggressively."

PREVIOUS DIAGNOSES AND TESTING RESULTS

[In this section you can list previous diagnoses and past testing.]

LEGAL STATUS/HISTORY

[Describe custody, legal history, and current legal status here.]

FAMILY CONSTELLATION

David and Lisa Axehandle are Biff's parents. His older sister, Linda, currently attends Loogie College in Redbud, Minnefornia. Mr. and Mrs. Axehandle are both employed and live in a suburban area outside of Redbud, Minnefornia.

DEVELOPMENTAL HISTORY

[Key elements include a well-written and comprehensive narrative that includes elements that will be discussed later under risk and protective factor headings. Strengths and weaknesses should both be included. A key aspect is that this is the author's opportunity to lead the reader through the youth's life so that when they come to the "recommendations" section they have likely come to the same conclusions as the author. This is also an opportunity to transmit an understanding of the youth's view of the world as well as the experiences that led to his theories of how things are in the world.]

FAMILY HISTORY

[Relevant information goes here, including any family history of mental health, sexual abuse, or substance abuse problems. Strengths and weaknesses can both be addressed.]

PSYCHIATRIC HISTORY

Biff has an extensive history of involvement with mental health services, with varying levels of response. Primary themes have included his poor peer interactions and physical aggression towards others. Pharmacological interventions have been an important part of his treatment to date, and a history of his medications is provided below.

[A key aspect is what is the young person's history of psychiatric/mental health treatment and how did he respond to interventions?]

PLACEMENT HISTORY

[This is self-explanatory.]

Biff lived with his parents until the age of 14, at which time the New Seaport Department of Child Protective Services (CPS) placed him in foster care. After seven months, Biff's foster parents contacted CPS to state that his behavior problems precluded further placement in their home. Biff was subsequently placed at the St. Nicholas Home in Brass River, Calisota. While at Brass River, Biff sexually assaulted his roommate (described below), and upon investigation it was revealed that he had… Biff was admitted to the New Seaport Youth Academy on ____.

SCHOOL HISTORY

As noted above, Biff began to have social and emotional difficulties at or before pre-school. He was administered psychological evaluations in 1990 and 1993, with both evaluations indicating functioning in the average range of intelligence. Biff has spent his school career identified as learning disordered and educationally handicapped. More recently, he has been diagnosed with disorders of _____.

A Psychological Evaluation dated ___ yielded WISC-III scores of

____. A more recent evaluation dated ___ and using the ___ found Biff to be in the low average range, with scores lower than in his earlier years. This report also notes "an inability to maintain satisfactory interpersonal relationships."

MALTREATMENT HISTORY

[Relevant history regarding the youth's own victimization, neglect, and other trauma can go here.]

SEXUALLY ABUSIVE BEHAVIOR HISTORY

Biff met with this writer on ___ and ___. He was informed of the limits of confidentiality and the purpose for this report. Upon admission, Biff acknowledged involvement in inappropriate behavior, and a need for treatment in this area. He has since acknowledged that the incidents at his previous placement were coercive in nature. Five conduct reports from the St. Nicholas Home were provided to this writer, with excerpts included below.

Biff states that the first sexual contact he can remember was when he was seven or eight. This apparently occurred on one occasion in the basement of a neighborhood house with a boy named Scooter who was younger than Biff. He says that this included touching the other boy's penis, [describe any self-report here]. He later stated that he and the other boy made attempts to engage in anal sex. Biff states that he made it clear to Scooter that he was not to tell anyone of their activity, but that Scooter told his mother and that the police interviewed him. He does not recall any further actions taken.

Biff further describes engaging in sexual contact with a different younger boy in the neighborhood whose name he does not recall. He describes very similar incidents of rubbing, touching the other boy's penis, and attempts to engage in anal sex. As with the other boy, Biff is very unclear on what specific threats he used or actions he took to ensure that this contact remained secret. However, he acknowledges making it very clear to each boy that they were not to tell. He states that the incidents between himself and these boys took place approximately 3 or 4 times with each boy.

Biff states that between the time of these incidents and his admission to the St. Nicholas Home, he had consensual vaginal intercourse with two or three same-age young women who he considered girlfriends. He insists that no coercion was involved and that these were the result of friendly and caring relationships. His parents report no knowledge of these young women.

As noted above, Biff was admitted to the St. Nicholas Home for the 1991-1992 school year, just prior to his fifteenth birthday. The following incidents are excerpted from the record:

August 2, 1991: A student reported that Biff had entered his room and started a conversation. The conversation became increasingly personal, with Biff offering to take him for a ride in his car at the holidays. Biff reportedly began to rub his chest and back, gradually pulling down the student's pants. At that point the student apparently told him to stop and he did. Biff reportedly told the student not to tell. The student reportedly waited two weeks, and expressed a concern that Biff would be angry at him.

February 5, 1992: A staff reported that he found Biff performing oral sex on another student. An addendum dated ___ stated that this incident had been reported to CPS and that an investigation was underway by the Sheriff's Department.

March 2, 1992: A student reported that Biff reportedly tried to hug him and wrestle his pants off. The student told Biff he had to go to an appointment, got out of Biff's grasp, and left the room.

May 8, 1992: A student reported that Biff had entered his room the previous night, pulled down his pants and fondled his penis and buttocks. The student told Biff to stop and Biff left the room.

Biff has since acknowledged the coercive nature of these incidents. He states that in many of these cases, he had considered his actions for months prior to the events, where consideration included selecting someone who wouldn't fight back and who might be willing. He has stated that he was angry with others for various reasons at the time of the latter incidents, and that he had been involved in many arguments with his parents.

According to a letter to ___ from ___, there was a report of Biff sexually assaulting a five-year-old in his neighborhood (no victim gender is provided). Apparently there was no follow-up to this allegation at the time of the report. In conversations, Biff's mother does not recall an incident of this nature, although she acknowledges an awareness of other incidents described above.

COURSE OF PLACEMENT/MOST RECENT INCIDENTS

[An overview of the youth's response to treatment can be inserted here. For purposes of example, we will imagine that he has been involved in incidents of both violence and sexual aggression towards others.]

Biff was recently involved in incidents in which he attempted to sexually assault a younger, more vulnerable peer and aggressively propositioned an adult male staff member… [Include dates and details.]

IMPRESSIONS

A possible limitation of this report is that no self-report inventories mapping attitudes and beliefs around sexual behavior were used. Rather, this report is based on Biff's work in treatment and observable behaviors within the milieu. I am concerned that his learning disabilities and cognitive abilities would obscure the results of these scales.

Also, no physiological measures such as the penile plethysmograph, visual reaction time, or polygraph were used. However, in Biff's situation, I feel that each would be of limited utility. Biff is young, and his developmental level could contribute to uncertain results with each measure. Measures such as the polygraph and plethysmograph may also be counterproductive to treatment due to their potentially intrusive nature. Further, sexual interest and arousal patterns as measured physiologically can be quite fluid and dynamic across adolescence (Hunter & Becker, 1994). Additionally, although Biff targeted younger boys in each recent instance, it can also be argued that his choice was based more on availability and detection than sexual preference. It is also possible that given Biff's level of functioning, these younger boys are closer to his developmental level and functioning than others of his age. For this reason, along with the fact that his thoughts and contact with them were short-lived, he does not currently meet the criteria for pedophilia.

Even without these measures, however, Biff has a clearly established pattern of willingness to engage in sex with others, potentially of both genders, who are unwilling or appear likely to offer little resistance. His motivation, by all appearances, has been more to establish himself as powerful and engage in sex than to obtain gratification from humiliating others. While he presents himself as streetwise and threatening, and resorts to aggression when he perceives threat, there is very little evidence of his actively seeking to humiliate others in his daily life. Although adults working with sexual abusers will want to screen for sexual sadism in many situations, Biff does not meet the criteria for this diagnosis, or for Paraphilia, NOS, nonconsent, at this time (see Doren, 2002).

Many factors appear to influence Biff's patterns of behavior. The first is his self-reported perception that he is not like others. He is clearly frustrated both by his differences from same-age peers, as well as his skin condition. He feels alienated from the surroundings that he wants to be a part of (including his own family and community). Given Biff's age and developmental status, it is of little surprise that Biff does not experience remorse or empathy in the ways that most adults do. However, there is evidence that these can develop, particularly in the context of treatment, in the future (Siegel, 1999). Biff does, however, experience considerable shame, and expects very little from his own future.

Currently, there is no empirically validated method for assessing Biff's risk for future harmful sexual behavior. However, the following historical risk factors, based on recent research, suggest an elevated level of risk:

- Biff has persisted in coercive sexual contact despite detection by adults, moderate sanctions (removal from his previous program and placement in another) and the first stages of a course of treatment targeting harmful sexual behavior.
- Biff's victims are unrelated.
- Biff has a conviction for a violent nonsexual offense (simple assault).

Also of concern is the early onset of Biff's aggressive behavior towards others, although it is noted that he has not been diagnosed with Conduct Disorder in any of the records cited above.

Dynamic (and potentially changeable) risk factors that suggest an elevated level of risk include:

- *A sense of sexual entitlement evident in his behavior and self-report.* At the time of the above incidents, Biff was apparently not concerned with the impact or consequences of his actions. He reports that he was simply interested in obtaining sexual gratification by whatever means available. His reported consideration of these acts for several months in advance suggests that this sense of sexual entitlement is of significant concern to those working with Biff.

- *Emotional loneliness.* Biff has a lack of emotionally intimate relationships, and a history of difficulty in creating these relationships. This is an area of some salience to Biff, who experiences a sense of loneliness very frequently.

- *Poor problem-solving skills.* Biff is able to solve problems for himself in low-stress circumstances. However, when he is upset, angry, or anxious, it is very difficult for him to anticipate problems or generate alternatives to problem behaviors such as physical or sexual aggression.

Protective factors that may mitigate Biff's risk include:

- His family's support for treatment.

- His long-standing acknowledgement of a need for treatment.

- His demonstrated willingness to engage in treatment.

- His willingness to learn new ways to develop and maintain relationships.

- Elements of a pro-social orientation. Although Biff postures and presents himself as threatening, he quickly loses interest in these elements of his life when given the opportunity to work or enjoy one-to-one time with supportive adults. This is most apparent in pre-vocational education situations.

SUMMARY AND RECOMMENDATIONS

Biff is a sixteen-year-old young man who has faced significant challenges across much of his life to date. These range from ___ to ___ and ___. They also include long-standing behavioral problems, and psychiatric difficulties. Although he states that his primary sexual interests are towards age-appropriate females, he has a historical willingness to engage in sexual contact with males significantly younger and more vulnerable than himself. Although this appears to reflect those who are available to Biff, it is also of obvious concern to future treatment providers. Although he possesses many attitudes tolerant of aggression, he has little demonstrated interest in other forms of antisocial activity, and is easily engaged in pro-social activities under optimal circumstances. Biff is amenable to treatment but displays a pattern of behavior that has persisted despite detection, the threat of sanction, and the beginnings of treatment. He does not meet the criteria for a sexual disorder at this time, although this should be reviewed should he continue to engage in harmful sexual behaviors. At present, he might best be viewed as a young man whose ability to form appropriate relationships based on respect and empathy has gone badly awry due in large part to his life circumstances. Despite these challenges, Biff's behaviors should not be understood as intractable or without amenability to change.

At the same time, Biff remains in need of the intensive level of supervision and structure found in a residential treatment center. Due to his assaults on a _____ and a ___, Biff requires a higher level of care than that available at the New Seaport Youth Academy. It is recommended that he be placed in another setting that can manage his behavior while providing opportunities for carefully supervised education oriented towards vocational skills building.

_____   _____

Raven Desktop, LCSW   Date

Fancy title goes here

REFERENCES AND RESOURCES

[It can be useful and instructive to include references. This can include those provided within the text of the report as well as any additional references or resources that may be helpful to future assessors or treatment providers.]

APPENDIX B

Juvenile Risk Assessment References
Compiled by Phil Rich and David Prescott

Alexander, M. (1999). Sexual offender treatment efficacy revisited, *Sexual Abuse: A Journal of Research and Treatment, 11*, 101-116.

American Academy of Child and Adolescent Psychiatry. (1999). Practice parameters for the assessment and treatment of children and adolescents who are sexually abusive of others. *Journal of the American Academy of Child and Adolescent Psychiatry, 38:* 12 (Suppl. December), 55s-76s.

Becker, J. V., & Kaplan, M. S. (1988). The assessment of sexual offenders. *Advances in behavioral assessment of children and families, 4,* 97-118.

Becker, J. V., Kaplan, M. S., Cunningham-Rather, J., & Kavoussi, R. J. (1986). Characteristics of adolescent incest sexual perpetrators: preliminary findings. *Journal of Family Violence, 1,* 85-97.

Becker, J. V., & Harris, C. (2004). The psychophysiological assessment of juvenile offenders. In G. O'Reilly, W. L. Marshall, Carr, A., & R. Beckett (Eds.), *The Handbook of clinical young people who sexually abuse* (pp. 191-202). Hove, England: Brunner-Routledge.

Beckett, R. (1999). Evaluation of adolescent sexual abusers. In M. Erooga & H. Masson (Eds.), *Children and young people who sexually abuse others: Challenges and responses* (pp. 204-224). London: Routledge.

Bremer, J.F. (2001) The Protective Factors Scale: assessing youth with sexual concerns. Plenary address at the 16th annual conference of the National Adolescent Perpetration Network, Kansas City, Mo. May 7, 2001.

Borum, R., Bartel, P., & Forth, A.E. (2002). *Manual for the structured assessment of violence risk in youth.* Tampa, Florida: University of South Florida. Available at http://fmhi.usf.edu/.

Calder, M. C. (2001). *Juveniles and children who sexually abuse: Frameworks for assessment* (3rd ed.). Dorset, England: Russell House Publishing.

Calder, M. C. (Ed.). (2000b). *The complete guide to sexual abuse assessments.* Dorset, England: Russell House Publishing.

Calder, M. C. (2000a). The comprehensive assessment of juveniles who sexually abuse. In M. C. Calder (Ed.), *The complete guide to sexual abuse assessments* (pp. 73-88). Dorset, England: Russell House Publishing.

Caldwell, M. (2005, May). *What we do and do not know about juvenile sex offenders.* Presentation at the annual conference of the Wisconsin Association for the Treatment of Sexual Abusers, Madison, WI.

Caldwell, M.F. (2002). What we do not know about juvenile sex offense risk assessment. *Child Maltreatment, 7,* 291-302.

Campbell, T. W. (2004). *Assessing sex offenders: Problems and pitfalls.* Springfield, IL: Charles C. Thomas.

Eldridge, H. (2000). Patterns of sexual offending and strategies for effective assessment and intervention. In C. Itzen (Ed.), *Home truths about child sexual abuse: Influencing policy and practice* (pp.313-334). London: Routledge.

Epperson, D. L., Ralston, C. A., Fowers, D., & Dewitt, J. (2005, February). *Optimal predictors of Juvenile sexual recidivism in a large scale study of Utah adolescents who have offended sexually.* Paper presented at the 20th Annual Conference of the National Adolescent Perpetration Network, Denver, CO.

Forth, A.E., Kosson, D.S., & Hare, R.D. (2003). *Psychopathy Checklist: Youth Version.* Toronto, Ontario, Canada: Multi-Health Systems.

Gilgun, Jane F., Klein, C., & Pranis, K. (2000). The significance of resources in models of risk, *Journal of Interpersonal Violence, 15,* 621-650.

Graham, F., Richardson G., & Bhate, S. (1997). Assessment. In M. S. Hoghughi (Ed.), *Working with sexually abusive adolescents* (pp.52-91). Thousand Oaks, CA: Sage.

Grisso, T. (1998). *Forensic evaluation of juveniles.* Sarasota, FL: Professional Resource Press.

Grisso, T. (2003).*Massachusetts Youth Screening Instrument – Version 2.* Sarasota, FL: Professional Resource Press.

Grisso, T., Barnum, R., Fletcher, K. E., Cauffman, E., & Peuschold, D. (2001). Massachusetts youth screening instrument for mental health needs of juvenile justice youths. *Journal of the American Academy of Child and Adolescent Psychiatry, 40,* 541-548.

Hanson, R.K. (1997). The development of a breif actuarial risk scale for sexual offense redivism. Department of the Solicitor of Canada, Ottawa, Ontario.

Hanson, R.K., & Harris, A.J.R. (2001). A structured approach to evaluating change among sexual offenders. Sexual Abuse: *A Journal of Research and Treatment,* 13(2), 105-122

Henggeler, S.W., Schoenwald, S.K., Borduin, C.M., Rowland, M,D., & Cunningham, P.B. (1998). Multisystemic treatment of antisocial behavior in the children adolescents. New York7 Guilford Press.

Hoge, R D., & Andrews, D. A. (1996). *Assessing the youthful offender: Issues and techniques.* New York: Plenum Press.

Hoge, R.D., & Andrews, D.A. (2003). *Youth Level of Service/Case Management Inventory.* Toronto, Ontario, Canada: Multi-Health Systems.

Hudson, S. M., & Ward, T. (2001). Adolescent sexual offenders: Assessment and treatment. In C. R. Hollin (Ed.), *Handbook of offender assessment and treatment* (pp. 363-377). Chicester, England: John Wiley.

Hunter, J. A. & Lexier, L. J. (1998). Ethical and legal issues in the assessment and treatment of juvenile sexual offenders. *Child Maltreatment, 3,* 339-348.

Hunter, J. A., & Becker, J. V. (1999). Motivators of adolescent sexual offenders and treatment perspectives. In J. A. Shaw, J. A. (Ed.). *Sexual aggression* (pp. 211-233). Washington, DC: American Psychiatric Press.

Hunter, J.A., Figueredo, A.J., Malamuth, N.M., & Becker, J.V. (2003). Juvenile sex offenders: Toward the development of a typology, *Sexual Abuse: A Journal of Research and Treatment, 15,* 27-48.

Kenny, D.T., Keough, T., & Seidler, K. (2001). Predictors of recidivism in Australian juvenile sex offenders: implications for treatment, *Sexual Abuse: A Journal of Research and Treatment, 13,* 131-148.

Knight, R. A. (2004). Comparison between juvenile ad adult sexual offenders on the multidimensional assessment of sex and aggression. In G. O'Reilly, W. L. Marshall, Carr, A., & R. Beckett (Eds.), *The Handbook of clinical young people who sexually abuse* (pp. 203-233). Hove, England: Brunner-Routledge.

Lane, S. (1997a). Assessment of sexually abusive youth. In G. Ryan & S. Lane (Eds.), *Juvenile sexual offending: Causes, consequences, and correction* (new and rev. ed.) (pp. 219-263). San Francisco, CA: Jossey-Bass.

Langstrom, N., & Grann, M. (2000). Risk for criminal recidivism among young sex offenders, *Journal of Interpersonal Violence, 15,* 855-871.

Lee, J. K. P., Jackson, H. J., Pattison, P., & Ward, T. (2002). Developmental risk factors for sexual offending. *Child Abuse & Neglect, 26,* 73-92.

Loss, P., & Ross, J. E. (1988). *Risk assessment/interviewing protocol for adolescent sexual offenders.* New London, CT: Authors

Marczyk, G.R., Heilbrun, K., Lander, T., & DeMatteo, D. (2003). Predicting juvenile recidivism with the PCL:YV, MAYSI, and YLS/CMI, *International Journal of Forensic Mental Health, 2,* 7-18. Available at http://www.iafmhs.org/files/Marczyk.pdf.

McCann, J. T., & Dyer, F. D. (1996). *Forensic assessment with the Millon inventories.* New York: Guilford.

McCann, J. T. (1998). *Malingering and deception in adolescents: Assessing credibility in clinical and forensic settings.* Washington, DC: American Psychological Association.

National Task Force on Juvenile Sexual Offending. (1993). The revised report on juvenile sexual offending, 1993 of the National Adolescent Perpetration Network. *Juvenile & Family Court Journal, 44,* 1-120.

Nisbet, I.A., Wilson, P.H., & Smallbone, S.W. (2004). A prospective longitudinal study of sexual recidivism among adolescent sex offenders. *Sexual Abuse: A Journal of Research and Treatment, 16,* 223-234.

O'Brien, M. J. & Bera, W. (1986, Fall). Adolescent sexual offenders: A descriptive typology. *Preventing Sexual Abuse, 1* (3), 1-4.

O'Reilly, G. & Carr, A. (2004). The clinical assessment of young people with sexually abusive behavior. In G. O'Reilly, W. L. Marshall, Carr, A., & R. Beckett (Eds.), *The Handbook of clinical young people who sexually abuse* (pp. 161-190). Hove, England: Brunner-Routledge.

Perry, G. P., & Orchard, J. (1992). *Assessment & treatment of adolescent sex offenders*. Sarasota, FL: Professional Resource Press.

Poole, D., Liedecke, D., & Marbibi, M. (2001). *Risk assessment and recidivism in juvenile sex offenders: A validation study of the static 99*. Austin, TX: Texas Youth Commission.

Prendegrast, W. E.(2004) *Treating sex offenders: A guide to clinical practice with adults, clerics, children, and adolescents* (2nd ed.). Binghampton, NY: Haworth.

Prentky, R. A, & Edmunds, S. B. (1997). *Assessing sexual abuse: A resource guide for practitioners*. Brandon, VT: Safer Society Press.

Prentky, R., Harris, B., Frizzell, K., & Righthand, K. (2000). An actuarial procedure for assessing risk with juvenile sexual offenders. *Sexual Abuse,A Journal of Research and Treatment 12*, 71-93.

Prentky, R. & Righthand, S. (2003). Juvenile Sex Offender Assessment Protocol – II (JSOAP – II). Available from Center for Sex Offender Management at www.csom.org.

Prescott, D.S. (2005). Emerging strategies for assessing risk : Theory, controversy, and practice. In R. Geffner, K.C. Franey, T.G. Arnold, & R. Falconer (Eds.). *Identifying and treating youth who sexually offend: Current approaches, techniques, and research*. Binghamton, NY: Haworth Press.

Rasmussen, L.A. (1999) Factors related to recidivism among juvenile sexual offenders, *Sexual Abuse: A Journal of Research and Treatment, 11*, (1), 69-86.

Rasmussen, L., Burton, J., and Christopherson, B. (1992). Precursors to offending and the trauma outcome process. *Journal of Child Sexual Abuse, 1* (1), 33-48.

Rich, P. (2003). *Understanding juvenile sexual offenders: Assessment, treatment, and rehabilitation*. Hoboken, NJ: John Wiley & Sons.

Righthand S., & Welch, C. (2001, March). *Juveniles who have sexually offended: A review of the professional literature.* Washington, DC: Office of Juvenile Justice and Delinquency Prevention, U. S. Department of Justice.

Righthand, S., Prentky, R., Knight, R., Carpenter, E., Hecker, J.E., & Nangle, D. (2005). Factor structure and validation of the Juvenile Sex Offender Assessment Protocol (JSOAP). *Sexual Abuse: A Journal of Research and Treatment, 17,* 13-30.

Ross, J., & Loss, P. (1991). Assessment of the juvenile sexual offender. In G. D. Ryan & S. L. Lane (Eds.), *Juvenile sexual offending: Causes, consequences, and correction* (pp. 199-251). Lexington, MA: Lexington Books.

Sciarra, D. T. (1999). Assessment and treatment of adolescent sex offenders: a review for a cross-cultural perspective. *Journal of Offender Rehabilitation, 28* (3/4), 103-118.

Smith, W. R., & Monastersky, C. (1986). Assessing juvenile sexual offenders risk for re-offending. *Criminal Justice and Behavior, 13,* 115-140.

Vizard, E. (2002). The assessment of young sexual abusers. In M. C. Calder (Ed.), *Young people who sexually abuse: Building the evidence base for your practice* (pp. 176-195). Dorset, England: Russell House Publishing.

Will, D. (1999). Assessment issues. In M. Erooga & H. Masson (Eds.), *Children and young people who sexually abuse others: Challenges and responses* (pp. 86-103). London: Routledge.

Worling, J.R. (2001). Personality-based typology of adolescent male sexual offenders: differences in recidivism rates, victim-selection characteristics, and personal victimization histories, *Sexual Abuse: A Journal of Research and Treatment, 13,* 149-166.

Worling, J. (2002). Assessing risk of sexual assault recidivism with adolescent sexual offenders. In M. C. Calder (Ed.), *Young* people who sexually abuse: Building the evidence base for your practice (pp. 365-375). Dorset, England: Russell House Publishing.

Worling, J.R. (2004). The Estimate of Risk of Adolescent Sexual Offense Recidivism (ERASOR): Preliminary psychometric data. *Sexual Abuse: A Journal of Research and Treatment, 16,* 235-254.

Worling, J.R., & Curwen, T., (2000). Adolescent sexual offender recidivism: success of specialized treatment and implications for risk prediction, *Child Abuse and Neglect, 24,* 965-982.

NEARI Press Titles

The NEARI Press
New England Adolescent Research Institute
70 North Summer Street
Holyoke, MA 01040
Phone (413) 540-0712

Current Perspectives: Working with Sexually Aggressive Youth and Youth with Sexual Behavior Problems by R. E. Longo & D. S. Prescott (Editors)(2006). NEARI Press. **ISBN# 1-929657-26-9**

Enhancing Empathy by Robert E. Longo and Laren Bays (1999). NEARI Press. Paperback, 77 pages.
ISBN#1-929657-04-8

Growing Beyond by Susan L. Robinson (2002). NEARI Press. Paperback, 216 pages. **ISBN# 1-929657-17-X**

Growing Beyond Treatment Manual by Susan L. Robinson (2002). NEARI Press. Paperback, 42 pages.
ISBN# 1-929657-15-3

Lessons from the Lion's Den: Therapeutic Management of Children in

Psychiatric Hospitals and Treatment Centers by Nancy S. Cotton, Ph.D. (2005). NEARI Press. Paperback, 354 pages. **ISBN# 1-929657-24-2**

Men & Anger: Understanding and Managing Your Anger by Murray Cullen and Robert E. Longo (1999). NEARI Press. Paperback, 125 pages. **ISBN#1-929657-00-5**

Moving Beyond Sexually Abusive Behavior: A Relapse Prevention Curriculum by Thomas F. Leversee (2002). NEARI Press. Paperback, 88 pages. **ISBN# 1-929657-16-1**

Moving Beyond Student Manual by Thomas F. Leversee (2002). NEARI Press. Paperback, 52 pages.
ISBN# 1-929657-18-8

New Hope For Youth: Experiential Exercises for Children & Adolescents by Robert E. Longo & Deborah P. Longo (2003). NEARI Press. Paperback,150 pages. **ISBN# 1-929657-20-X**
Paths To Wellness by Robert E. Longo (2001). NEARI Press. Paperback, 144 pages. **ISBN#1-929657-13-7**

Power Struggles: A Book of Strategies for Adults Who Live and Work with Angry Kids. by Penny Cuninggam (2003). NEARI Press. Paperback, 112 pages. **ISBN# 1-929657- 23-4**

Respecting Residential Work With Children by James R. Harris (2003). NEARI Press. Hardcover, 163 pages.
ISBN# 1-929657-21-8

Strong at the Broken Places: Building Resiliency in Survivors of Trauma (2005).by Linda T. Sanford. NEARI Press. Paperback, 208 pages. **ISBN# 1-929657-25-0**

The Safe Workbook for Youth by John McCarthy and Kathy MacDonald (2001). NEARI Press. Paperback, 210 pages. **ISBN# 1-929657-14-5**

Who Am I and Why Am I In Treatment by Robert E. Longo with Laren Bays (2000). NEARI Press. Paperback, 85 pages. **ISBN#1-929657-01-3**

Why Did I Do It Again & How Can I Stop? by Robert E. Longo with Laren Bays (1999). NEARI Press. Paperback, 192 pages. **ISBN#1-929657-11-0**

Using Conscience as a Guide: Enhancing Sex Offender Treatment in the Moral Doamin by Niki Delson (2003). NEARI Press. Paperback, 102 pages. **ISBN# 1-929657-22-6**

Using Conscience as a Guide: Student Manual by Niki Delson (2003).
NEARI Press. Paperback, 50 pages.
ISBN# 1-929657-28-5

~ ~

For prices and shipping information, or to order, please call:
Whitman Distribution 800.353.3730

Find us on line at: www.neari.com